Prodigal

ALSO BY LINDA GREGERSON

POETRY

Fire in the Conservatory (1982)

The Woman Who Died in Her Sleep (1996)

Waterborne (2002)

Magnetic North (2007)

The Selvage (2012)

CRITICISM

The Reformation of the Subject (1995)

Negative Capability (2001)

Empires of God, coedited with Susan Juster (2011)

Prodigal

New and Selected Poems,
1976–2014

LINDA GREGERSON

Mariner Books
Houghton Mifflin Harcourt
Boston   New York

ACKNOWLEDGMENTS

The Kenyon Review: "The Wrath of Juno (A wandering husband),"
"Heliotrope," "The Dolphins," "The Wrath of Juno (It's the children)"

The New Yorker: "Ceres Lamenting"

Poetry: "Sostenuto," "The Weavers"

Poetry Review (London): "Pythagorean"

Raritan: "Font," "And Sometimes"

Fire in the Conservatory was first published by Dragon Gate Press.

The Woman Who Died in Her Sleep, Waterborne, and *Magnetic North* were first
published by Houghton Mifflin Company.

The Selvage was first published by Houghton Mifflin Harcourt.

Kind thanks to my editors: Gwen Head, Peter Davison, Pat Strachan, Janet
Silver, Michael Collier, Jenna Johnson. To David Baker and Rosanna Warren,
astute counselors. To Steven Mullaney, first reader and occasional (reluctant)
persona in these poems. To Emma and Megan. And to my sister Karen. This
book is for her.

For information about permission to reproduce selections from this book,
write to Permissions, Houghton Mifflin Harcourt Publishing Company,
215 Park Avenue South, New York, New York 10003.

www.hmhco.com

Library of Congress Cataloging-in-Publication Data is available.
ISBN 978-0-544-30167-2

Book design by Greta D. Sibley

Printed in the United States of America
DOC 10 9 8 7 6 5 4 3 2

K. A. Gregerson
1954–2014

CONTENTS

New Poems

Sostenuto

Night. Or what

                     they have of it at altitude
like this, and filtered
         air, what was

in my lungs just an hour ago is now
         in yours,
                  there's only so much air to go

       around. *They're making
more people,* my father would say,

          but nobody's making more land.
                  When my daughters
were little and played in their bath,

         they invented a game whose logic
largely escaped me —
           something to do with the

             disposition
of bubbles and plastic ducks — until
       I asked them what they called it. They

were two and four. The game
was Oil Spill.
    Keeping the ducks alive, I think,

        was what you were supposed to
      contrive, as long
as you could make it last. Up here

    in borrowed air,
in borrowed bits of heat, in costly
      cubic feet of steerage we're
a long

    held note, as when the choir would seem
to be more
    than human breath could manage. In

      the third age, says the story, they
divided up the earth. And that was when
    the goddess turned away from them.

The Wrath of Juno

(Echo)

          A wandering husband
     peopling the earth
with my humiliations

          which
     the narrative requires.
At least I shall never

          be out of work.
     I'm not immune
to loveliness myself, in fact,

          especially
     in the warmer months,
so much of it on display: the young

          ones in their pretty
     summer dresses and their open
shoes, new crops of them every year.

          I simply think
     the better choice, what makes
for dignity all round, is not

          to touch.
     But try telling that to a
man who thinks he's a shower of gold.

What mystifies me,
truly, are the ones who guard
the door. Nothing at stake

but vague
contempt for playing-it-all-
too-straight. You'll have heard

the girl's affliction—
can't stop talking, can't
say anything original—

was something
I did to her after the fact.
But look where she started.

And listen to what's
become of me.

The Weavers

As sometimes, in the gentler months, the sun
will return
                    before the rain has altogether
                                   stopped and through

this lightest of curtains the curve of it shines
with a thousand
                    inclinations and so close
                                   is the one to the

one adjacent that you cannot tell where magenta
for instance begins
                    and where the all-but-magenta
                                   has ended and yet

you'd never mistake the blues for red, so these two,
the girl and the
                    goddess, with their earth-bred, grass-
                                   fed, kettle-dyed

wools, devised on their looms
transitions so subtle no
                    hand could trace nor eye discern
                                   their increments,

yet the stories they told were perfectly clear.
The gods in their heaven,

           the one proposed. The gods in

                  heat, said the other.

And ludicrous too, with their pinions and swansdown,
fins and hooves,

           their shepherds' crooks and pizzles.

                  Till mingling

with their darlings-for-a-day they made
a progeny so motley it

           defied all sorting-out.

                  It wasn't the boasting

brought Arachne all her sorrow
nor even

           the knowing her craft so well.

                  Once true

and twice attested.
It was simply the logic she'd already

           taught us how

                  to read.

Font

At the foot of the download anchored
                    among
          the usual flotsam of ads,

this link: to plastics-express.com who for
                    a fraction
          of the retail price can

solve my underground drainage woes, which
                    tells me
          the software has finally

run amok. Because the article, you see,
                    recounts
          the rescue from a sewage

pipe of Baby 59, five pounds,
                    placenta still
          attached, in Zhejiang

Province, where officials even as I read
                    are debating
          the merits of throwing

the mother in jail. Communal
                    toilet. Father
          nowhere to be found.

The gods in their mercy once
                        could turn
            a frightened girl to

water or a shamed one to a tree,
                        but they
            no longer seem

    to take our troubles much
                        to heart.
            And so the men with

hacksaws do their gentle best—consider
                        the infant
            shoulders, consider the lids—

and this one child among millions,
                        delivered
            a second time to what

we still call breathable air, survives
                        to pull
            the cords of sentiment

and commerce.
                        Don't make the poem
            too sad, says Megan,

thinking at first (we both of us
                                    think) the child
                        must be a girl or otherwise

damaged, thus (this part she doesn't
                                    say) like her.
                        Who is the ground

of all I hope and fear for in the world.
                                    Who'll buy?
                        Or as the hawkers

on the pavement used to put it, What
                                    d'you lack?
                        The download comes with

pictures too. Of workmen, wrenches,
                                    bits of shattered
                        PVC, and one for whom

the whole of it—commotion, cameras,
                                    IV needle in the scalp—
                        is not more strange

than ordinary daylight.
                                    Welcome, Number
                        59. Here's milk

from a bottle and here's a nearly
                                    human hand.

The Dolphins

You think these powers began with you?

We were men before this happened.
We could run
                    and stand. We couldn't drink

the water but we built the ships that made it link
us up: salt-rich
                    head of family to your query strings

and URLs. Why,
having charted the heavens, should we bother
                    with the gods?

The boy was a deliberate trap, I see that now.
The delicate
                    bridge between shoulder

and breastbone. The not-quite-having-wakened
bit of stagger
                    when he walked. And

tears, that lovely pooling at
the lower lid
                    the instant before they dropped

and then the dropping, when he saw how far
from shore we'd come.
                And all of it

staged, so he could watch the panic when
our hands
                began to flatten into flippers.

Is there something you love about yourself?
Some here-
                I-am-articulate?

And then to lose it, joint by joint.
It's that
                that left me with this rictus

of a mouth and with the thing he no doubt
flatters himself
                by calling understanding.

Once, to show his power, the god of ivy
spread
                his mantle on

the shouldering waves, till even the waters
smothered.

The Wrath of Juno

(the house of Cadmus)

It's the children nail your heart
to the planet, so that's
           how you nail them back.
          Alcmena in labor

for seven days. Think of the man
who thought up the goddess
          who thought of that.
          And pregnant

Semele, stupid with pride, consumed
by the flames she had the gall
          to ask for, though
          I ought to have known

that wouldn't be the end of it. *Who'll
rid me of the turbulent mess that comes
          attached to a womb?*
          That's always been

their fantasy. As witness Minerva,
sprung from his head. Or Dolly the sheep,
          or IVF. Or this one,
          absurdly

sewn up in a thigh. *Not only have you long*
outlived your function, you
                    were never required
                    in the first place. Still,

I have my ways. In this particular
instance, the child was finally born as a god,
                    I couldn't touch him.
                    But we're not

a race best known for our restraint.
If you're willing to think on a larger scale,
                    there'll always be an angle.
                    Some

bright child of a child of the single
house that sponsored all my torment.
                    Whose
                    sweet skull plates hadn't

a chance in the world against that rock.
You invented me, brother, now
                    you have to live with me.

Heliotrope

(Olivier Theatre, South Bank)

I was his favorite, simply that.
                And you can see

for yourself why it might have been so:
                the lushest, least

likely to weary the eyes of all
                the serried wavelengths.

Never obvious.
                My bit

of the spectrum unstable somehow,
                in a way that kept

bringing him back. Search
                image

on your browser and you'll see
                what I mean.

I've never had the advantage of
                sculptural

beauty, as the lily has, I haven't
                been able to boast

that stricture of line. That making-
                no-mistakes. God

knows I've wished for it, beggars
                can dream.

But no. Some neither-this-nor-
                that turns out to be

my sphere. Some manyness rather
                than singular

perfection. Which I like to think
                he thought about.

He made this place.
                They named it

for him. And upholstered the seats
                in *heliotrope,*

whose cluster of vowels and con-
                sonants

he loved like my blue-going-violet-
                with-touches-of-

gray. The vocal colors. Warm-up,
                nightly, before

the play. So you see, they were
		wrong, the ones

who called me unrequited. I
		was in his throat,

among the folds and ridges and
		beyond them to

the very dome upon whose curve
		the heart resides.

Just think what it used to be then,
		in the hour before

they'd let the rest of you in:
		my many faces toward

the sun who spoke—no, sang—
		my name.

Pythagorean

Square of the square of the
                    root
          that holds it all together, maybe the geometricians

were right. Or maybe
                  it's music after all,
          the numbers in their other incarnation, makes

the planets make us what we are,
                  which means
          in turn

the parts I learned in Tunis and at Delphi must
                  be surface
          agitations on a deeper pool.

Talk to me, won't you,
                  what was it like
          in your other life?

It came to me all at once that day:
                  the dog
          being beaten, the voice of my friend

in the dog.
                  I'd had
          the thought before sometimes, or something

next door to it, watching them
                                    slaughter the ox
           for food. Who'd pulled

the plow in fellowship.
                            How strange
           we need these turnings-against

before we're allowed to see.
                            And when
           you think of it, isn't it strangeness

that's the problem in the first place? I
                            who ought
           to be at home here in these hips

and bowels and neuro-
                            navigations flat-
           out baffled by the genius of it all and then

offended when it starts to fail.
                            Or starts, I should say, to
           mark a path

that isn't in my interest.
                            Does my brother the ox
           decide to be slit with a knife?

Oh I know what a crank
                    they've taken me for, my
        railing against the carnivores, spoiling

the party, tainting the wine
                    with blood.
        I don't know

what I will be or what I should call the thing
            I am,
        but I know what I used to be.

Ceres Lamenting

I.

For Emma's three samples
of landrace maize,
        the blue, the red,
the long-toothed yellow, my uncle

reserved
just east of the barn a plot
        as yet
unpoisoned by the pesticide

which the cranes, who are also
endangered, unerringly
        found
so when

the first green shoots had sprouted
they were one
        by one
before their time extracted

from the earth and seed by seed
consumed.
        When everything else
had gone to hell—

rich men jumping from windows and
the whole
                    of Oklahoma turned
to dust—this farm,

this godsent
quarter section and a half, was like
                    a fence against
confusion. Now

we say to the children, This fenceless
world . . .

        2 .

She hated the plow.
She hated the cattle.
                She hated
that her sweet acres when the girl

had been taken away should still
contrive to be
                    conformable, even
the barley, even the grape, as though

her heart had not been torn
with hooks.
                Well if they
could be reckless so could she.

And that was when
the blighted times we live in first began,
            the dying rivers and
the blackened vine,

the rain that rots the seed in its furrow,
the spavin, the sheep scab,
            the empty hive.
And even in the midst

of this calamity the girl,
who was so young you see, had room
            in her heart to be sorry
about the lilies and the sage.

    3.

Last night too—do all
of our stories begin with rape?—the girl
            came back
from the dead somehow. The crowbar,

the bus, the whole
ungodly mess of it lit and scripted on a
            stage
and we could tell

it wasn't quite business as usual, wasn't
the thing
            we thought we'd bought
our tickets for. The actors, yes,

were lovely to look at, all but one,
which made
                    the truth and rightness part
go down like milk. But then

the one with the ruined face began to speak
and *(kerosene)*
                    (dowry) then the damage
wasn't safely in its grave.

And all this while
the cunning
                    counterargument kept seeping
its way back in, no help for it, every

decision they'd made — the words,
the few bare things assembled
                    on the floor — informed
with shapeliness, even

the anger, even the grief.
Which may
                    be what they meant,
the old ones: up

to our elbows in wreckage, and April
forever refusing
                    to be ashamed.

And Sometimes,

thank heaven, the question includes
        a layer
    of real delight.

The youngest recruit in the lab—it's why
        we need them—had
    the freshest thought: a

box, a wooden hammer, and a two- or even
        four-year-old child,
    it didn't seem to matter, and

the chimp whatever age the chimp might
        happen to be.
    You get quite fond of them,

needless to say, it tends to distort the data.
        But in this
    we felt quite pure, that is,

the leaning (*I am like you* and
        I like this)
    was built in, we thought. Hypothesized.

And so we seemed to prove. You simply
                teach them to open
            the box: rap once with the hammer

(the chimp would be more adept at this) then
                slide a bolt and presto:
            lift the lid. No

punishment, no moral, just
                this happy accession of
            able-to-make-the-whole-thing-work.

I wish he'd found
                that sort of pleasure, my
            good friend, before he died. *I sleep,*

I wake up, I don't
                know what it means, he said.
            Which left the poor young doctor

quite outside his realm of competence.
                He taught me much, my
            friend, not least

what fierceness really looks like, but
                I must be made
            of thinner stuff. Or luckier, if

loving the answer we got from the box
            is luck.
      The hammer, you see, and bolt

are unrelated to the lifted lid,
            mechanically speaking,
      as making the box transparent makes

transparent (second phase), and if you've
            guessed
      where this is going then

you've caught the twinkle
            in God's blue eye.
      The chimp in the space of a heartbeat

went directly
            for the lid whereas
      the human child would keep, if

that's the word for it, the whole
            of the sequence
      she'd learned to think essential. She

or he, that is, it didn't seem to matter.
            So
      the hammer, bolt and, as

she had been taught, the lid. My sister
                   once spent
              a year of her life

learning to use a *voltage clamp,*
                        it's something to do
              with cell walls and their methods

of letting the outside in.
                        And coming
              from my sister's voice I almost

understand it. Not
                        a single path but many,
              the forms of devotion, I mean.

The part that makes us human more
                   clusive
              than we'd thought.

FROM *Fire in the Conservatory*

How Love, When It Has Been Acquired,
May Be Kept

That was when the war was on, the one we felt good
to hate, so of course I thought he'd come from there.
It was June. The light grown long again.
She'd roll his chair to the window

and back. But no, you said, it was love.
They were getting it wrong.
A leg. A leg. An arm to the elbow.
Like the man who burned his daughter to get

good winds. The sea for days had been flat
as the sky. He'd walk while the light went down
and could only tell the water from the air by the drag
below his knees. So this is what it's like

to have no body. A perfect benevolent temperature.
The wheels of the chariots grind
in the hulls of the ships. He lay so still he honeycombed,
may he be safe, may we be sound. The time

they bargained for came piece by piece.

Indications That One's Love Has Returned

There's an illness, of the sort that's named for a man
who first imagines that disparate threads might be threads
on a loom, that is called his syndrome, and frightens
the weaver, who cannot unravel by night

what she sees in the day. Their table had the sun for hours.
The piazza was white. They talked
about physicians at home, whose stories were longer, if less
in accord. And about the morning months ago

when the color first spread beneath her eyes.
From cheekbone to cheekbone, the smallest vessels had burst
in a pattern called *butterfly*, they'd named that too,
as the tour guides name rocks till you can't see the sandstone plain

anymore, but Witch's Cauldron and Hornet's Nest.
The wings went away. The course of the river that carved the rock
is air now, and baffles intent. She'd been used to a different notion
of course, the kind you might follow for love of the thing

or of knowledge, the wings in the glass.

Geometry

What I like best about the snowplow is morning
then night, but anyway without the sun.
I drive from town to old 16 and back again, wider.
The sound I make's all mine, like the tunnel from the headlamps,
mine. First I plow with the light and then with the plow.
The best part closes up behind. I could tell you but I won't
how the farms separate, each one packed around a single light
for prowlers or company. The light that's modern and blue
stops farther out and sharper than the yellow kind. I'd as soon
steal a chicken in blue. Where the highway makes a triangle
with 16 and county O, a picnic table bellies up.
The tracks fill in. When I wake sometimes
I don't know the room, there's nothing to see by
and nothing to see if I could. The fields
are parceled into squares by roads named for letters
but who could know it in the dark?
Anyone can be here when the night thins out.

Maudlin; Or, the Magdalen's Tears

If faith is a tree that sorrow grows
and women, repentant or not, are swamps,

a man who comes for solace here
will be up to his knees and slow

getting out. A name can turn on anyone.
But say that a woman washes the dust

from a stranger's feet
and sits quite dry-eyed in front

of her mirror at night.
The candle flame moves with her breath, as does

the hand of the painter, who sees in the flame
his chance for virtuosity. She lets him leave

her shoulder bare.
Bedlam's distilled from a Mary too,

St. Mary's of Bethlehem, shelter
for all the afflicted and weak

of mind. The donors conceived of as magi
no doubt. The mad and the newborn

serve equally well for show.
A whore with a heart, the rich

with a conscience, the keepers of language
and hospitals badly embarrassed at times

by their charge. The mirror refuses
the candle, you see. And tears on another's behalf

are not
the mirrors he's pleased to regard.

Who loves his ironies buxom and grave
must hate the foolish water of her eyes.

Wife

I've had a couple the oblique way,
you know, the one he's not with now,
now he's with me. Both of them were dark,

isn't that funny, and taller than I am.
A voice you'd be pleased to have,
or go home to, though different

on that point, I don't mean to overgeneralize.
Very unique, as my neighbor once said of several
houses in Baltimore. Their voices

were distinct, I'd say. Both good.
The one ran fresh in the middle of words, and clotted
round the consonants. You'd never need dessert.

The other had the tone of hand-rubbed wood,
rows of tasteful bindings. In the head, your own,
something happens to timbre,

like singing in the shower, we're better
for what gets trapped. Spells caution for my vanity,
since I like what I've heard here too,

if the voice is some version of color onstage,
translated by gels,
but not the way the wheel I learned

would lead me to expect. Or the versions
of his memory: the one who was splendid
in front of the fire, the one who got old fast,

the one who could cook.
Can you tell when the reed in the throat
has split? How does the sentence go then?

Much Missed

The indiscriminate light comes home
and the sailor comes home from the sea,
who could link his thoughts of her sweet white thigh

to any business at hand. He returns
to blue candles on a chocolate cake, the flickering tokens
of her regard. It's strength of lung

that floats a wish. *The dark one's breasts used to melt*
when she stretched. Reach me the ashtray, I'd say,
and never let on what I watched when she did. Here

and gone. She never gave me trouble at night.
Here's love in a cup,
his Penelope says. May it speed you back
to me.

2.

Some of this is morning fog and some of it
afternoon. The event somehow escapes her.
City much missed

by landlocked exiles, now
that she's here, she still makes her way by rumor
and the clock. *I can hear the water rising*

in your sleep, the separate strands
of raveled breath. Lies down to work,

takes walks in honor of an absent guide.
The tree in the lungs, the bishop pine, these great stiff rattles
protesting the wind.

    3.

The wind that year blew the topsoil away, and salt
came up the river. Toby came up from town.

Toby with the running eyes and a cane that'd put the fear of God
into any dog
came up from town to be fed, and was, and died

one night when the weather changed.
Not enough breath to cloud the mirror. And later
some woman who came for his shoes. *What did you do?*

We hoped for rain.

Fire in the Conservatory

The panes of glass arrived by boat
and sat in boxes for a year,
the man with the mansion in San Jose having died.
The workmen paid from a public collection had never seen

Cape Horn, though one of them loved
the wind through his scaffold, the fog
at its legs, and imagined the moorings might loosen
before they were done. He and the People's Crystal Palace

out to sea, his lunch in its box
attracting an escort of gulls. When the plants moved in,
Mr. Giles of the inspiration at Kew
dispatched a gift: seeds from the Royal Water Lily

sailed with a cargo of hemp through the Golden Gate, as once
down the Nile, up the Thames,
and, musing several seasons away, again
obliged with three-foot leaves. *Royal* for *big,*

or to show whose river counted most,
or because such leaves make the water a pavement
for any man's feet.
The birds of paradise squawked in their bowls.

Observe the plush mouths of dependency. The lily
squandered its blossoming on two
successive nights;
the caretaker's boys lit a road's length

of lanterns, and public officials
launched candles in paper boats: they all moved west.
The fog, remember. The carriage wheels.
The ladies' guild with a plaque. The children

slept for the most part, preferring
the parrot who lived in the central dome, who amused them
by biting the gardener's hose, who rolled a bright eye
and nursed a black tongue.

"Halfe a Yard of Rede Sea"

(Corpus Christi pageant, c. 1574)

An afterthought? When all but one
of the glovers or joiners who signified

Red Sea had been sewn
fine caps for ready

identification? Or was it thriftily
cut in two and hung

on staffs that parted to let God's
people go through? The waters dividing

were not more mute
about their ways and means than this

account book entry made
four hundred years ago. *A wall*

on the right, a wall on the left.
We know the hours a man would spend

assembling chamois or lengths of wood
to earn the sixpence that bought

the sea. We know as well as he how white
the hand appears that harms those bent

on harming us.
Gratitude's been brief

as Pharaoh's softened heart for longer
than his rue, so books

parcel memory: this I've paid,
this I owe. Though bread lie plentiful

as dew, the people shall measure
the portion they eat, and want

what the past looks like from here
as half a yard of sea might want

the moon. *The wilderness
hath shut them in.* The players in red

are looking the other way. And the mind
must reckon with waters that have no

mind to open or heal so legibly
again.

FROM *The Woman Who Died in Her Sleep*

The Bad Physician

The body in health, the body in sickness,
inscribing
its versatile logic till the least

of us must, willy-nilly, learn
to read.
And even in error, as when

the mutant multiplies, or first
my right eye,
now my left, is targeted

for harm by the system
designed
to keep it safe,

even in error the body
wields cunning
as birches in leaf wield light.

The child who swallows the amnion now
will swallow milk
by winter. The milk

can find a use for me but not
for my belief,
nor yours, and it beggars the best

of our purposes. Within us
             without us,
      this life is already beyond us,

so what must it make of the man who cures
             by rote?
      My friend's young daughter moved

with a slightly muddied
             gait,
      and then her tongue

and then her hands
             unlearned
      their freedom, so newly

acquired. Unlearned with great
             labor
      while the tumor thrived,

and all the elixirs in Mexico
             could not
      revise her sentence by a day.

You who make your living at
             the body's re-
      versible deviations,

what will you say to a six-
        year-old
    when all her bright first lessons

are defaced? Even the skeptic
        in his lab,
    who works at the friable boundaries

of our common
        legibility
    and does the work that I trust

best, is bound to frame his question
        in the pure,
    distorting light of hope.

The beautiful cells dividing have
        no mind
    for us, but look

what a ravishing mind
        they make
    and what a heart we've nursed

in its shade, who love
        that most
    which leaves us most behind.

For My Father, Who Would Rather Stay Home

No deadfall in these woods of yours.
                    No
hollowed-out trunks.

No needy,
                    unseemly
          hanging on, as puts

a man with a chainsaw
                    to shame.
          The row of rusting oildrums and the

spavined Ford are nearly
                    obscured
          by sumac and scrub,

whose thin-legged plans for the future
                    outrun
          all reasonable grounds for hope.

It's ground you never meant
                    to give.
          If bracken

wants to euphemize an un-
             regenerate
       combine and a heap

of salvaged pipe,
             it works
       its homely camouflage unbidden

and unblessed.
       The Ford
       might lend you parts someday, and woe

betide the nesting squirrels
       who've taken
       to its deep front end. Life

is exactly long
             enough,
       except for the thin-skinned

or beggarly
             daughters,
       who haven't struck your bargain

with the pure hard edge
       of luck.
       Remember when we planted the Norway

pine? Five hundred seedlings
                the first
        year and not one of them made

full growth. No light.
                Or scant
        light, what the grudging oaks

let through. What you love
                best
        shall be taken away

and taken away in the other
                life too,
        where you haven't got

a stand of oak at all,
                old man,
        nor three winters' cordwood,

nor work for the heart,
                nor hapless
        daughters

to mortgage everything up.
                You think
        I haven't gathered how

the world divides?
            The un-
        stanched, unrequited lapse

of time has been your
                quarrel
        since before I learned to

temporize, till every other
                word's
        goodbye. It shouldn't be

too much to ask, this
                dying
        on familiar ground, but look

at the bracken, keeping
                the ground
        in place. You who don't

reproach me
                reproach me
        with failing to see,

as though a traveler,
                finding
        the inn a pleasant one,

should lose his way.
        The way
    you have in mind makes mine

digression, but
        while age
    may be your privilege, it's

no alibi.
        The parable
    means absent without leave,

you see. I'll keep you
        as long
    as the woods are deep,

and then I'll let you go.

Safe

(K. M. S. 1948–1986)

I.

The tendons sewn together and the small bones
        healed, that your hand
        might close on a pencil again

or hold a cup. The delicate muscles made
        whole again,
        to lift your eyelid and govern your smile,

and the nerves new-laid in their tracks.
        The broken
        point of the kitchen knife—and here

let the surgeon be gentle—removed and the skull
        knit closed
        and the blood lifted out of the carpet and washed

from the stairs. And the nineteen-year-old burglar returned
        to the cradle or
        his mother's arms, he must have been harmless

once, even he, who is not sorry, had
        nothing
        to lose, and will never be harmless again.

2.

Emma is learning to wield her own spoon—
                 silver for abundance,
          though it seldom finds her mouth as yet.

She hates to be fed, would rather starve,
                 but loves
          to steer the precarious course herself.

Silver for pride, then, or luck of the sort
                 some children
          are born with, omitting

the manifold slippage
                 that separates
          privilege and weal. Luck in this popular figure

is three parts silver anyway,
                 that the child
          not succumb to crack in the schoolyard,

rats in the hall, the clever fence with a
                 shopping list,
          bad plumbing, bad food, and hatred-on-a-staircase

with a knife in hand and dim designs
                 on jewelry
          or a VCR. The spoon was superfluity—

the best part of your paycheck for a child
        you haven't lived
           to see. Friend, her cheek is fresh as hope

of paradise. And every passing minute in the hours
        of light
           and the hours of darkness, in the fever

of pneumonia or the ignorant sweet wash
        of health,
           the miraculous breath

moves into her lungs and, stitch
        by mortal
        stitch, moves out.

        3.

When the paramedics came at last, my friend
        apologized:
           she must have hit her head, she thought,

she'd just take a minute to mop up the mess
        by the phone.
           Her broken hands, for which

the flaw in memory had provided no such
        alibi,
           her broken hands had kept him two or

three times from her face.
            And later,
       when the anesthesiologist had

launched her on his good green gas
            and launched her,
       as they do sometimes, a shade too fast,

she slipped the bonds of recall altogether.
            Safe
       as houses. You know what a house is for the likes

of us: downpayment on the nursing home,
            our foursquare
       pledge to be debtors of conscience, if debtors

in conscience may not look too closely
            where credit's
       refused. Our piece of the here for here-

after, which shows us diminished regard
            and just
       such a face as fear has made:

one night a woman came home to her house
            and locked its useless
       locks, and buttoned her nightdress and read

for a while, and slept till she was wakened.

An Arbor

1.

The world's a world of trouble, your mother must
          have told you
     that. Poison leaks into the basements

and tedium into the schools. The oak
          is going the way
     of the elm in the upper Midwest—my cousin

earns a living by taking the dead ones
          down.
     And Jason's alive yet, the fair-

haired child, his metal crib next
          to my daughter's.
     Jason is nearly one year old but last

saw light five months ago and won't
          see light again.

2.

Leaf against leaf without malice
          or forethought,
     the manifold species of murmuring

harm. No harm intended, there never is.
                    The new
            inadequate software gets the reference librarian

fired. The maintenance crew turns off power one
                    weekend
            and Monday the lab is a morgue: fifty-four

rabbits and seventeen months of research.
                    Ignorance loves
            as ignorance does and always

holds high office.

            3.

Jason had the misfortune to suffer misfortune
                    the third
            of July. July's the month of hospital ro-

tations; on holiday weekends the venerable
                    stay home.
            So when Jason lay blue and inert on the table

and couldn't be made to breathe for three and a
                    quarter hours,
            the staff were too green to let him go.

The household gods have abandoned us to the gods
                    of juris-
            prudence and suburban sprawl. The curve

of new tarmac, the municipal pool,
            the sky at work
      on the pock-marked river, fatuous sky,

the park where idling cars, mere yards
            from the slide
      and the swingset, deal beautiful oblivion in nickel

bags: the admitting room and its stately drive,
            possessed
      of the town's best view.

            4.

And what's to become of the three-year-old brother?
            When Jason was found
      face down near the dogdish—it takes

just a cupful of water to drown—
            his brother stood still
      in the corner and said he was hungry

and said that it wasn't his fault.
            No fault.
      The fault's in nature, who will

without system or explanation
            make permanent
      havoc of little mistakes. A natural

mistake, the transient ill will we define
          as the normal
      and trust to be inconsequent,

by nature's own abundance soon absorbed.

     5.

Oak wilt, it's called, the new disease.
          Like any such
      contagion—hypocrisy in the conference room,

flattery in the halls—it works its mischief mostly
          unremarked.
      The men on the links haven't noticed

yet. Their form is good. They're par.
          The woman who's
      prospered from hating ideas loves causes

instead. A little shade, a little firewood.
          I know
      a stand of oak on which my father's

earthly joy depends. We're slow
          to cut our losses.

Good News

1.

The hobbled, the halt, the hasten-to-blame-it-on-
        childhood
    crowd, the undermined and over-

their-heads, the hapless,
        the humbugs,
    the hassle-me-nots. The night

before the night my uncle Jens
        saw Jesus
    standing in the hayloft, he—

my uncle Jens, that is—considered
        cashing the whole
    thing in. Bettina gone

the way she had, the boys all gone
        to hell . . .
    The mild flat light of evening lay

like a balm on the fields. But for his heart
        no balm
    in sight. So Jens

gave all his money to the local charis-
        matic,
    and in exchange his fellow faithful told him

to forgive himself. God's god-
    forsaken children
  all over the suburbs and the country-

side are dying in the service
    of a market
  share. Witness

the redhead I used to go to college with,
    who played
  the trombone and studied Kant and now

performs the laying on of hands somewhere
    in eastern
  Tennessee. Beneath her touch

quenched sight returns, the myelin sheath
    repairs
  and lets the wheelchair rust, the cancerous

cat comes purring back to health.
    But Jens,
  whose otherworldliness imperfectly

cohered, took to driving his pickup
    off the road,
  in desultory fashion for the most part,

so that cousin Ollie's cornfield took
    the brunt
  of harm. The hens

ran loose. And Jens, who in his mother's arms
              had leapt
          for joy and in towheaded youth had leapt

to favor in each tender heart, went weary
          to salvation.

          2.

Having learned from a well-meaning neighbor
              that death
          will not have her if Jesus

does first, my three-year-old daughter
              is scouring
          the visible world for a sign.

The other she's found in abundance—
              death on her
          dinnerplate, death in the grass—

and drawing just conclusions is beside herself
              with fear.
          "Most Englishmen,"

the Archbishop said smoothly, "are still residual
              Christians.
          We still need a clergy for funerals."

The televangelist's plexiglass pulpit,
              the crystal veil
          of his tears, assure us the soul is

67

transparent too. No stone can break
                nor scandal mar
        the radiant flow of video con-

version. Close now, closer
                than audio
        enhancement, the frictionless

story that washes us clean.
                Words dis-
        encumbered of contingency,

of history, of doubt. God's
                wounds,
        they swore, the old ones,

the believers, as now we swear by sex or shit.
                God's wounds,
        which failures of attention made.

For the Taking

And always, the damp blond curls
            on her temples
        and bountifully down to her shoulder blades,

the rich loose curls all summer mixed with sand
            and sweat,
        and the rare, voluptuous double

curve of her nether lip—most children lose
            that ripeness before
        they can talk—and the solemn forehead,

which betokens thought and, alas
            for her, o-
        bedience, and the pure, unmuddied line

of the jaw, and the peeling brown shoulders—
            she was always
        a child of the sun . . . This

was his sweet piece of luck, his
            find,
        his renewable turn-on,

and my brown and golden sister at eight
            and a half
        took to hating her body and cried

in her bath, and this was years,
        my bad uncle did it
   for years, in the back of the car,

in the basement where he kept his guns,
        and we
   who could have saved her, who knew

what it was in the best of times
        to cross
   the bridge of shame, from the body un-

encumbered to the body on the
        block,
   we would be somewhere mowing the lawn

or basting the spareribs right
        outside, and—how
   many times have you heard this?—we

were deaf and blind
        and have
   ever since required of her that she

take care of us, and she has,
        and here's
   the worst, she does it for love.

The Resurrection of the Body

for Caroline Bynum

She must have been thirteen or so, her nascent
        breasts
    just showing above the velcro strap

that held her in her chair.
        Her face
    translucent, beautiful,

as if a cheekbone might directly render
        a tranquil
    heart. And yet

the eyes were all dis-
        quietude.
    The mother with her miraculous

smile, frequent, durable, lifted
        the handkerchief—
    you know the way a woman

will?—her index finger guiding a corner,
        the body of it gathered
    in her dextrous palm—and with

such tenderness wiped the spittle
        pooling
    at her daughter's mouth. The faint

warm smell of lipstick—remember?—freighted
   with love,
  and with that distillate left by fear

when fear's been long outdone by fearful
    fact.
  The mother would give her soul to see

this child lift her head on her own.
    And down
   the hall in orthotics,

I couldn't for the longest time understand
    why the boy
  required a helmet so complexly fitted

and strong—his legs were unused, his arms
    so thin.
  A treadmill, I thought. Or a bicycle maybe, some

bold new stage of therapy anyway, sometimes
    he falls
  and, safe in his helmet, can bravely

set to work again. It wasn't for nothing
    that I was
  so slow. Who cannot read these waiting rooms

has so far—exactly so far—been spared.
        It was only
    while I was driving home,

my daughter in her car seat with her brand-
        new brace,
    that I thought of the boy's rhythmic rocking

and knew. Green light. Yellow. The tide
        of pedestrians
    flush and smooth. And the boy's

poor head against the wall—how could I miss it?
        and what
    does God in his heaven do then?—the boy's

poor head in its bright red helmet knocking—
        listen—
    to be let in.

Bunting

"They're sleeping," said Emma, "they're very
           tired,"
    as the footage came on again,

child after child in the chalk
          embrace
    of chemical death. We saw again

the elegant economy with which God
           sculpts
    the infant face. Not one

not cast in heaven's mold.
          Not one
    —and how could this be true?—dis-

figured by what brought them here,
          by death
    throe and the bland assimilations

of the evening news, by lunatic cal-
          culation
    or malevolence, which launched the gas,

by money, which made it
            and made as well
      the sumptuous ground rhythm

that supplants the children on the screen,
          lures Emma
      full front now and wants her to want

with the whole heart of childhood what
           money
      will buy. The patron's deft

technologies. Our sponsored
          view.
      The cutting-room distillations that can take

our breath away. The man
         in the dust
      and the child in its unearthly

beauty, still in his arms, they're
          Kurds,
      they fell as they ran.

2.

Megan woke up at three last night,
         cold
      and wet and frightened till we made

her warm. We had clean nightclothes.
        We had
    clean sheets. Plentiful water runs

from the taps. Megan believes that someone's
        in charge
    here. Megan thinks love

can make you safe. In Vu-
        kovar,
    in our world, in nineteen ninety-one,

they're cutting off limbs with no
        anesthesia,
    the people have lived in cellars

for eighty-six days. And where there's
        no food
    there's a microphone, and in

the fallen city there's a woman's voice:
        "They have not
    won. We do not hate them. We will

not hate them as they hate us."
        But I must
    have misunderstood the first time,

or understood in a clearing somehow, no
        head
    for the trees. Because two

days later I heard the words in another
        voice, a man's
    voice now, and filtered through trans-

lation: "We do not hate them.
        They have
    not made us animals."

He, you understand, was on the other side.
        And both
    of them had the same rumor for proof.

"Unconfirmed," unthinkable,
        on both sides
    the harrowing goes like this:

We—we're like you—we protected the children,
        even while the mortars
    made rubble of our town. They

left forty-seven children lying with their
        throats cut
    on the schoolroom floor.

3.

Faster than thought, or the kind that still seems to us
          human,
    faster than fear or the flaring neuron, upward,

now toward us, now dazzlingly
        away,
    the missile describes in liquid fire

its deadly, adaptable notion of
        home
    and makes a sort of conscript of the midnight sky.

Silicon matrix, father
        land.
    The groundlings in their gas masks need some ground

for hope, but hope's the very substance of dispute,
        and who
    will draw its boundaries? Here

is the man of seventy-four whose heart quite foolishly
        stopped,
    though the sirens went off for no reason

that time. Here is the infant
        who smothered.
    It seems that the valves on the breathing device

can be turned the wrong way. Here
   is the mother
  who turned them. The missile-seeking missile is

a Patriot, and see how the camera loves it.
    Heart
  hard-wired to a mobile launcher,

faithlessness keeping the software
    true.
  No wonder there's confusion on the homefront.

This isn't the shelter we thought we'd
    bought,
  who've wrapped the child in bunting,

rocked her in the cradle of the state.

Salt

Because she had been told, time and
        again,
          not to swing on the neighbors' high hammock,

and because she had time and again gone
        back, lured
          by the older boys and their dangerous

propulsions, because a child in shock (we
        didn't know
          this yet) can seem sullen or intran-

sigent, and because my father hated his life,
        my sister
          with her collarbone broken was spanked

and sent to bed for the night, to shiver
        through the August
          heat and cry her way through sleep.

And where, while she cried, was the life he
        loved?
          Gone before she was born, of course,

gone with the river-ice stored in sawdust,
    gone with the horses,
   gone with the dogs, gone with Arvid Anacker

up in the barn. 1918. My father was six.
    His father thought Why
  leave a boy to the women. Ole (like "holy"

without the h, a good Norwegian
    name)
  Ole had papers to sign, you see,

having served as county JP for years—
    you
  would have chosen him too, he was salt

of the earth—and Arvid's people needed to cut
    the body down.
  So Ole took the boy along, my father

that is, and what he hadn't allowed for was
    how badly
  Arvid had botched it,

even this last job, the man had no luck.
    His neck
  not having broken, you see, he'd thrashed

for a while, and the northeast wall of the barn—
        the near wall—
    was everywhere harrows and scythes.

It wasn't—I hope you can understand—
        the
    blood or the blackening face,

as fearful as those were to a boy, that, forty
        years later,
    had drowned our days in whiskey and dis-

gust; it was just that the world had no
        savor left
    once life with the old man was

gone. It's common as dirt, the story
        of expulsion:
    once in the father's fair

lost field, even the cycles of darkness cohered.
        Arvid swinging
    in the granular light, Ole as solid

as heartwood, and tall . . . how
        could a girl
    on her salt-soaked pillow

compete? The banished one in the story
        measures
    all that might heal him by all

that's been lost. My sister in the hammock
        by Arvid
    in the barn. I remember

that hammock, a gray and dirty canvas
        thing,
    I never could make much of it.

But Karen would swing toward the fragrant
        branches, fleshed
    with laughter, giddy with the earth's

sweet pull. Some children are like that,
        I have one
    myself, no wonder we never leave them alone,

we who have no talent for pleasure
        nor use
    for the body but after the fact.

Creation Myth

(Wheel-thrown stoneware, Richard DeVore)

I.

If the lines are not lovely in two
                dimensions,
        they'll never be lovely in three,

he said. The skirt will not hang right,
                the actress
        will stumble and blur.

And so my friend spent eighteen months
                on the floor
        with her scissors, through headache

and handcramp, recalcitrant muslins, and gavel-
                to-gavel
        coverage of the hearings that traced

a two-bit break-in straight
                to the President's
        heart. Democracy, the hem

of your garment. We had not loved you half
                so well
        had we not loved ineptly.

Till hand could feel and eye behold
      the seam
        between pattern and in-the-round,

the lip, just blade upon blade of her shears,
      converting
        clutter to a world of grace.

And then she learned the damasks and silks.
      And then
        she learned to light them.

    2.

The child does not walk at a year
      and a half,
        nor stand without prompting, nor

speak. The kindly professionals plot
      a curve
        that somehow will not rise as it should.

Please give, say the folding chairs,
      give,
        say the charts, please give oh give,

says the mother, a sign. The father
      has not come
        with her, this isn't the business

he meant it to be. Please give, say the child's
            sweet shoulders,
        a sign, and I will follow, I

will take the world for home.
            Isn't that
        the story you want? Wheel-thrown,

light-sown, God the potter moves his
            thumb,
        and what was motion now is

flesh, and still the child
            does not,
        according to our lights, thrive.

Cortex, medulla, ligament, gut—
            the least
        conductive membrane with its world

of wit. How dull we are on this scale
            and behind-
        hand in our praise. Dear

boy, in all your palpable
            beauty,
        you will have to teach us something we

should long ago have known
            by heart.

3.

In Norway he had worked with paint and
            lathe
and leafing, artisanal

orders that had no real equiv-
            alent
here, where they stole

his luggage and could or would not
            say
what it was his mild young

wife was soon to be dead of. But life
            was harsh
for so many back then.

He lettered signs and climbed
            the steeple
with gold for the cross and once,

for Mrs. Potter-Palmer's third-
            floor staircase,
copied a panel of wallpaper lately

plundered from a French chateau.
            And twice
on a Sunday (when else

could you paint the rotunda at Marshall
                    Field's?
          this was when people stayed home

after church) twice on a Sunday
                    he felt
          the hand of God directly.

Scaffolding broke that first time and he fell
                    thirty feet
          to be saved by shattering layers

of glass. Not a soul within ear-
                    shot and Lord
          what a wreckage of three-button

gloves. The second time he lost an eye.
                    What I
          remember is Oscar Nordby at eighty-

nine, rinsing his eye in an eyecup.
                    It must
          have been—don't you think so?—the good

eye, though from this distance I can't
                    be sure.
          The one was slightly yellow where the

white should be, and blue of course, and
the other,
glass. And always he knew

where the fault had lain.
Six days
labor and the seventh day rest,

to honor the father
who holds
a grudge. Eternity, the hem

of your garment. We had
not loved you
half so well had we not noted

what this grief is better than.
Do you see
where the glaze has roughened a bit

like human skin?
To honor
the father who made us.

With Emma at the Ladies-Only
Swimming Pond on Hampstead Heath

In payment for those mornings at the mirror while,
        at her
        expense, I'd started my late learning in Applied

French Braids, for all
        the mornings afterward of Hush
        and Just stand still,

to make some small amends for every reg-
        iment-
        ed bathtime and short-shrifted goodnight kiss,

I did as I was told for once,
        gave up
        my map, let Emma lead us through the woods

"by instinct," as the drunkard knew
        the natural
        prince. We had no towels, we had

no "bathing costumes," as the children's novels
        call them here, and I
        am summer's dullest hand at un-

premeditated moves. But when
        the coppice of sheltering boxwood
        disclosed its path and posted

rules, our wonted bows to seemliness seemed
poor excuse.
The ladies in their lumpy variety lay

on their public half-acre of lawn,
the water
lay in dappled shade, while Emma

in her underwear and I
in an ill-
fitting borrowed suit availed us of

the breast stroke and a modified
crawl.
She's eight now. She will rather

die than do this in a year or two
and lobbies,
even as we swim, to be allowed to cut

her hair. I do, dear girl, I will
give up
this honey-colored metric of augmented

thirds, but not (shall we climb
on the raft
for a while?) not yet.

Target

What is, says the chorus, *this human*
            desire—
do you know the part I'm

talking about? *What is this*
            human
            desire for children? Medea

has just left the stage
            (*ab-scaena,*
            said my friend, ob-

scene) to brood on her indelible work.
            His ety-
            mology is false, I've looked it up,

but my friend wasn't thinking
            of children
            in any case. What

says the mother, for all
            her books,
            who bathes the newborn child

in the sink, is sick
         with fear
     for the pulse in the scalp, the foot

still flexed as it was in the womb
        and peeling
     from the amnion. They have no death

in them yet, you see, their very excrement
        is sweet,
     they have no death but what's implied

in the porcelain rim, the drain
        with its food scraps,
     the outlet, the sponge, the thousand

mortal dangers in the kitchen drawer.
        I'd sometimes feel,
     with the child in my arms,

as I've felt looking down on the live
        third rail.
     What is this human desire

for children? They just make a bigger
        target
     for the anger of the gods.

2.

The thing she can't be rid of is that
                    no one
          would believe her. Not the uniformed

policeman at the edge of town (and surely
                    he knew her?
          the wildest boast of the census

could scarcely have amounted to
                    a decent
          row of pews on Christmas Eve),

nor her own forbidding father nor
                    good Emma
          at the kitchen sink. Months later

at the jury trial,
                    the word
          of a nine-year-old girl would suddenly

count. Late morning
                    on the third
          of May in 1929

(the other crash was yet to come),
                    no seam
          of comprehension in the ordered world,

no help from the mild
            spring sky,
        my nine-year-old mother ran at last

to the dead girl's house and de-
            livered
        her burden of blight directly. Arrow

unwilling, whoever took pity
            on you?
        The rest replays in borrowed

light: the courtroom in Chicago with its
            unswept floors,
        two girls with their handfuls

of violets. And one leaping one way while the car
            bore down
        and one, my mother, the other.

        3.

For those who think, as he did once,
            that in-
        advertent suffering is the worst of it here,

in the range between hating-thy-neighbor
            and destruction
        on a global scale, the middle range,

where people live, the range
                from the hills,
        the journalist decribes his con-

versation with a captured Serb.
                The boy—
        the man?—was twenty-two.

I am happy, he said. He must
                have been asked
        what he hoped for or thought

while he lay in the high half-light with his
                gun,
        a sniper in the frozen hills whose

angle on the heart and hearth's acute.
                I am happy,
        he said, *to kill a child crossing*

the street with his mother.
                Now something
        has been altered in the transit

from language to language, this isn't
                exactly
        the way we speak. Offstage,

obscene, the god-from-a-machine
        at work.
        And circuitry whose other name

is "happy": coincident
        access
        of never-on-this-good-green-earth

and ground-from-which-we-start.
        I am happy
        to kill a child crossing the street with his mother.

There is something so fantastic on the mother's face.

Bleedthrough

(Helen Frankenthaler, 1969)

I.

As when, in bright daylight, she closes
                her eyes
        but doesn't turn her face away,

or — this is more like it — closes her eyes
                in order
        to take the brightness in,

and the sunstruck coursing of blood through the
                lids
        becomes an exorbitant field to which

there is
                no outside,
        this first plague of being-in-place, this stain

of chemical proneness, leaves so little
                room
        for argument. You'd think

the natural ground of seeing when we see
                no object
        but the self were rage.

2.

My daughter has a trick now of composing
        her face
     and her shoulders and arms in a terrible be-

seeching shape—it all
        takes just
     the blink of an eye—I love

you, Mama, she says, I like
        this food,
     it's good, it's fine, I

can't even taste the burnt part, and she means
        Don't rain
     down fire again. She's nine.

And every penitent reparation—Do you like
        me, reader?
     Do you like me sorry now?—ensnares

her more and makes her shoulder
        more
     of this im-

partible estate. It seemed like
        Mars
     to me when I was young, that other

3.

world of women with its four fleshed walls
      of love.
        My mother, who can turn the most unlikely

raw materials to gladness, used
      to call
        her monthly blood "the curse." I

know, I know, our arsenal of pills
      is new,
        our tampons and detergents, all

our euphemizing gear; the body
      in even its
        flourishing seethes and cramps. When the

painter, for example, looks for
      leverage
        on a metaphor, nine-

tenths of her labor is in-the-flesh. The wash
      of acrylic,
        the retinal flare: we say

that the surfeited pigment "bleeds." And
      every
        counterargument—the margin of shoreline,

the margin of black, the four-
            fold
        margin she's stretched the canvas to com-

prehend—undoes itself a little in its straining after
            emphasis.
        I can tell, says my daughter, the difference between

        4.

the morning light and light at the end
            of the day.
        And from room to room in the crowded

museum she blazons her facility. That's night. That's
            not. That's
        Sunset Corner, says the plaque. As though

the vaults of fire had found their
            boundary
        in an act of wit, or California's amplitude

in glib suburban pavement. Or have I
            missed
        the point again? Outflanking

the painter's luxuriant brushwork
            (maybe
        I've loved this grief too well) is

something more quotidian and harder
        won.
            The fretted cloth on the third or fourth rinsing goes

yellow, goes brown, the young
        girl's hands
        —she's just pubescent—ache

with cold. Some parts—
        the red's
        bare memory now—were never bad. The sound

of the water, for instance, the smell,
        the rim
        of the stain that's last to go.

The Woman Who Died in Her Sleep

(Jeffrey Silverthorne, photographer)

1.

Not whipstitch nor blindstitch
                nor any
        sort of basting stitch I recognize, black

cordage, really, piercing its way from pubis
                to breast-
        bone—why not?—up to shoulder, the coroner's

question flatly left
                to the body's
        implacable gray. The part

in her hair is jagged too.
                Amazing
        what the flesh can make of all this in-

terruption. You've
                gathered
        that she's beautiful.

2.

When Megan chose the fifteenth-century sculpture
                rooms, I
        realized with some chagrin

she hadn't any notion who these
          people
      were. The one in blue,

I said, is Mary, and the one
          she's
      holding in her lap . . . till Megan

got the gist of it. And here,
          I said,
      is how you'll know him when they take

him down: five wounds. But my five-
          year-old
      daughter saw six. Have I

told you—do you know for yourself—how the
          sweetness
      of creation may be summed up in the lightfall

on a young girl's cheek? The wound
          she hadn't yet
      learned to ignore, the mortal one, was where

the child had once been joined
          to something else.

3.

She'd had worse news, the pale one, she'd felt terror
        sink
        its claw and hold, and never

had she lapsed into so lumpish
        a cliché.
        The bright young surgeon showed

her how to read the stark trans-
        parency,
        the telltale script of cells

gone wrong. And like some dull
        beginner
        she began to lose the edge of things

and had to sit (I'm
        sorry),
        had to drink some water (I'm

not like this, I can hear). The
        punishment
        for self-absorbed, she thought, is self-

absorbed. And all this black periphery
        is chiefly
        lack of blood flow to the

brain. Poor brain. It's body too.
              Is this,
         this old embarrassment, the way I'll know?

         4.

The woman in the photograph is
              lying
         on a pallet made of wood. And though

her abdomen appears to have been
              packed
         again in haste and though the breast

is badly sewn,
              her hips
         are smooth parentheses, her cheekbones

high, her lovely arms disposed as though
              in languor
         or luxurious thought. They took

my mother's teeth away—they had
              to, I can
         understand—the morphine I'd bullied them

into providing was meager
              and frequently
         late. And so my mother's face was not

the face I knew. But, reader,
                    her
          fine forehead was a blessing on the place.

The lesson, though I'm clumsy here, has something
                    to do

          5.

          with beauty and use.

The sculptors whose grammar my Megan
                    recites—
          a hole in each hand, a hole

in each foot, an entry
                    point
          beneath the breast—believed we get our

bodies back. And all the urgent calculus
                    that death
          can found and dis-

solution expedite was lavished in that era
                    on this one
          account:

What of the fingernails? What
                    of the hair?
          The menses? The milk? The proud-

flesh worn for heaven's sake?
              Who'd want,
         you see, the body oblivious?—body

on which the stern salt tide
              had left
         no mark? When Megan

hadn't yet been born—two months to go—
              my ankles swelled
         and doubled over every pair of shoes

I wore. Unseemliness, you seem
              to have some
         thing in mind. Imagine,

said the people once:
              a world
         where nothing is thrown away.

FROM *Waterborne*

Eyes Like Leeks

It had almost nothing to do with sex.
        The boy
           in his corset and farthingale, his head-

voice and his smooth-for-the-duration chin
        was not
           and never had been simply in our pay. Or

was it some lost logic the regional accent
        restores?
           A young Welsh actor may play a reluctant

laborer playing Thisby botching
        similes
           and stop our hearts with wonder. My young friend

—he's seven—touched his mother's face last night
        and said *It's*
        wet and, making the connection he has had

to learn by rote, *You're sad.*
        It's never
        not like this for him. *As if,*

the adolescents mouth wherever California spills
        its luminous
        vernacular. *As if,* until

the gesture holds, or passes. Let's just
             say
     we'll live here for a while. O

habitus. O wall. O moon. For my young
             friend
     it's never not some labored

simulacrum, every tone of voice, each
             give, each
     take is wrested from an unrelenting social

dark. There's so much dark to go around (how
             odd
     to be this and no other and, like all

the others, marked for death), it's a wonder
             we pass
     for locals at all. Take Thisby for instance:

minutes ago she was fretting for lack of a beard
             and now
     she weeps for a lover slain by a minute's

misreading. Reader, it's
             sharp
     as the lion's tooth. Who takes

the weeping away now takes delight as well,
which feels
for all the world like honest

work. They've never worked with mind before,
the rich
man says. But moonlight says, *With flesh*.

Noah's Wife

is doing her usual for comic relief.
                    She doesn't
          see why she should get on the boat, etc.,

etc., while life as we know it hangs by a thread.
                    Even God's
          had one or two great deadpan lines:

Who told you (this was back at the start
                    the teeth
          of the tautology had just snapped shut) *Who*

told you you were naked? The world
                    was so new
          that death hadn't been till this minute

required. *What makes you think* (the
                    ground
          withers under their feet) *we were told?*

The woman's disobedience is good for
                    plot,
          as also for restoring plot to human

scale: three hundred cubits by fifty
                    by what?
          What's that in inches exactly? Whereas

an obstinate wife is common coin.
                    In
            the beginning was nothing and then a flaw

in the nothing, a sort of mistake that amplified, the
                    nothing
            mistranscribed (it takes such discipline

to keep the prospect clean) and now the lion
                    whelps,
            the beetle rolls its ball of dung, and Noah

with no more than a primitive double-
                    entry audit
            is supposed to make it right.

We find the Creator in an awkward bind.
                    Washed back
            to oblivion? Think again. The housewife

at her laundry tub has got a better grip.
                    Which may
            be why we've tried to find her laughable,

she's such an unhappy reminder of what
                    understanding
            costs. Ask the boy who cannot, though

God knows he's tried, he swears
       each bar
         of melting soap will be his last, who cannot

turn the water off when once he's turned it on.
       His hands
       are raw. His body seems like filth to him.

Who told you (the pharmacopoeia has
       changed,
       the malady's still the same) *Who told you*

you were food for worms?
       What
       makes you think (the furrow, the fruit)

I had to be told?

Cord

(O. T. G. 1912–1994)

Dearest, we filled up the woodroom
        this week,
           Karen and Steven and I and Peter's

truck. You would have been amused
          to see us in our
       woodsman's mode. It's your wood still.

You know those homely cruxes where the odd piece,
          split
        near the fork, for instance, has to be turned

till it's made to fit and another
          lame one
        found for the gap? Sap

just yesterday, smoke in the end, this
          clubfoot
        marking the meantime. I came

to one of them, one of the numberless
          justnesses
        a life of stacking wood affords (had you even

broken rhythm?) and for just that instant
          had you back.
        I know. I know. It wasn't the last, despite

the strangled heaving of your chest, despite
       the rattled
    exhalation and the leavened, livid, meat-

borne smell, it wasn't the last till afterward, I've
       made that
    my excuse. But Mother was sleeping not five

feet away, she'd scarcely slept in weeks, I could
       have
    waked her. I (sweet darling, the morphine

under your tongue) am much (your quiet
       hands)
    to blame. And when we had dismantled this last-

but-one of the provident stores you'd
       left—
    a winter's worth of warmth in each—

and hauled it in, we split and stacked the new
       oak Peter
    felled last spring. We took a day off in

between, we wrapped ourselves in virtue, we
       can be
    good children yet. The gingkos

have come back from their near
                poisoning, have
      I told you that? Our tenant's

remorseful, he's sworn off new insecticides. My
                hour with you (one
      breath, one more) was theft.

Maculate

I remember going door to door, it must
          have been nineteen
    thirty-six and half the town was out of work,

we always had the Red Cross drive in March
          (*consider*
    the lilies how they grow). The snowmelt

frozen hard again, and cinders on the shoveled
          walks.
    I was wearing your grandmother's boots.

(*Consider the ravens, they have neither storehouse*
          nor barn.)
    The grocer gave a nickel, I can see him yet,

some people had nothing at all.
          And I came
    to Mrs. Exner's house (*no thief*

approacheth, neither moth). The woman
          was so bent
    with arthritis, nearly hooped

when she walked up the street with her bucket and mop
                (*not Solomon*
        in all his glory). The people

she cleaned for wouldn't keep a bucket in the house
                (*nor*
        moth). She gave me three new dollar

bills, I'll never forget it. I wanted the earth
                to swallow me up.

        2.

        Oilcloth on the kitchen table, linoleum

under his chair, and both of them an ugly hiero-
                glyphic
        of yellow scorchmarks ringed with black.

My father must be tired, to let the ash
                between
        his fingers and the still-lit butt-ends of his

days befoul the world around him so. Bone-
                tired
        and all but hammered to his knees

with drink. (*Burnt offering I have not required.*)
                The morning after
        the night he died (the undertaker's taillights

on the snow-packed drive), my mother sat just
                    there
          (*burnt offering I will not have*) and said

(*but only love*), I'm going to get a new kitchen floor.

          3.

                    The raven is not
          an unmixed consolation. What is manna

to the raven leaves a crust of blood
                    above
          its beak (*a treasure which no moth*

corrupts). The freckled lily festers. The unspotted
                    lily drops
          its trembling stamen in a smear of gold

(*laid up for thee*). And still it is no little
                    thing
          to think we shall be eaten clean.

The Horses Run Back to Their Stalls

It's another sorry tale about class in America, I'm sure
        you're right,
           but you have to imagine how proud we were.

Your grandfather painted a banner that hung from Wascher's
        Pub
           to Dianis's Grocery across the street: Reigh Count,

Kentucky Derby Winner, 1928.
        And washtubs filled
           with French champagne. I was far too young

to be up at the stables myself, of course, it took
        me years
           to understand they must have meant in *bottles*

in the washtubs, with ice.
        His racing colors
           were yellow and black, like the yellow

cabs, which is how Mr. Hertz first made the money
        that built
           the barns that bred the horses, bred at last this perfect

horse, our hundred and thirty seconds of flat-out earth-
        borne bliss.
           They bought the Arlington Racetrack then, and Jens

got a job that for once in his life allowed him to pay
                    the mortgage
          and the doctors too, but he talked the loose way even

good men talk sometimes and old man Hertz
                    was obliged
          to let him go. It was August when the cab strike in

Chicago got so ugly. Somebody must have tipped
                    them off,
          since we learned later on that the Count

and the trainer who slept in his stall had been moved
                    to another
          barn. I'll never forget the morning after: ash

in the air all the way to town and the smell of those
                    poor animals,
          who'd never harmed a soul. There's a nursery

rhyme that goes like that, isn't there? Never
                    did us any
          harm. I think it's about tormenting a cat.

Waterborne

The river is largely implicit here, but part
        of what
     becomes it runs from east to west beside

our acre of buckthorn and elm.
        (And part
     of that, which rather weighs on Steven's mind,

appears to have found its way to the basement. Water
        will outwit
     a wall.) It spawns real toads, our little

creek, and widens to a wetland just
        across
     the road, where shelter the newborn

fawns in May. So west among the trafficked fields,
        then south, then
     east, to join the ample Huron on its

curve beneath a one-lane bridge. This bridge
        lacks every
     grace but one, and that a sort of throwback

space for courteous digression:
        your turn,
    mine, no matter how late we are, even

the county engineers were forced to take their road
        off plumb. It's heartening
    to think a river makes some difference.

2.

Apart from all the difference in the world,
        that is.
        We found my uncle Gordon on the marsh

one day, surveying his new ditch and raining
           innovative
      curses on the DNR. That's Damn Near

Russia, since you ask. Apparently
        my uncle
    and the state had had a mild dispute, his

drainage scheme offending some considered
        larger
    view. His view was that the state could come

and plant the corn itself if it so loved
        spring mud. The river
    takes its own back, we can barely

reckon fast and slow. When Gordon was a boy
          they used to load
            the frozen river on a sledge here and

in August eat the heavenly reward—sweet
          cream—
            of winter's work. A piece of moonlight saved

against the day, he thought. And this is where
          the Muir boy
            drowned. And this is where I didn't.

3.

Turning of the season, and the counter-
          turn
            from ever-longer darkness into light,

and look: the river lifts to its lover the sun
          in eddying
            layers of mist as though

we hadn't irreparably fouled the planet
          after all.
            My neighbor's favorite spot for bass is just

below the sign that makes his fishing
          rod illegal,
            you might almost say the sign is half

the point. The vapors draft their languorous
excurses on
a liquid page. Better than the moment is

the one it has in mind.

Pass Over

I. PLAGUE OF DARKNESS

You point a camera at a kid, the kid
                will try
        to smile, he said. No matter part

of his mouth is missing, eyelid
                torn,
        the rest of his face such a mass

of infection and half-healed burns they'll
                never
        make it right again. You know

what the surgeon found in his scalp?
                Pencil lead.
        Six broken points of it, puncture wounds

some of them twelve months old. They figure
                the mother
        made him wear a ski mask for those

thousand-and-some-odd miles on the bus
                or why
        didn't somebody turn her in? The kid

is eight, the camera belongs to forensics, and
        he thinks
    he's supposed to smile. Do the math.

If anyone here were in charge, my vote is scrap us
       and start over.

2. PLAGUE OF FROGS

Indicator species is the phrase, I think.

Which means we pour our poisons in the streams
       and swamps
    and these poor creatures grow an extra

leg or lingual tumors or a cell wall so
       denatured
    that the larvae fail. In my new favorite

movie it begins as rain, a burst
       of guts
    and mucus on the hero's car, the hero

such as he is, poor man, who's lost
       his gun and now
    is lost himself before the windshield's slick

indictment, throat of frog, webbed foot
       of frog, split
    belly sliding down the glass in red

and yellow closeup, thence to join
      the carnage
    on the street, boot deep now, bred

of neither air nor water but of God's disgust
      with humankind.
    Behold them, said the prophet, in

thine ovens and thy kneading troughs. And
      then he said, Take,
    eat. This is the body you have made.

3. PLAGUE OF LOCUSTS

Because there's never enough. No, not
      in this bright
    field of surfeit: milk rings on the phone bill, tracked-in

honey where the cats came through, lost
      homework,
    last year's coggins on the tackroom floor.

My neighbor back in Somerville had only the
      narrowest
    path to walk, from table to toilet, toilet

to bed, the rest was floor to ceiling with what normal
      people throw
    away. I see how it comes to this. Never

enough of it battened down. I lose my pills, he said
        to me once,
           they're rolling around on the floor somewhere.

The Parsis bring their dead, as Zoroaster
        is construed
           to have taught them, to Malabar Hill, where

when the world was well the birds
        restored them
           to simplicity in ninety minutes flat.

The birds are purpose-built for this, their scabrous
        faces bear
           a nearly paraphrastic kinship to the fetid

stuff they tunnel in. O who will come who will
        not choke?
           The birds cannot keep up.

4. HYSSOP, LAMB

Explain to me the writing on the doorposts,
        will you, now,
           while the angel gorges on them

and theirs, each that was first to open the
        matrix, first
           still matters in this first world,

that much I have seen and do in part
               acknowledge.
        Archived in the space behind the lintel

and its hasty script, a logic of division
            that has made
       the world articulate, a portal for each

fine discrimination of the covenanting
            mind.
       And heaven has its discards too, there's not

a book I know that tells me otherwise.
           I'm having
       trouble reading in this light though.

Was it something in the water, or before?

Narrow Flame

Dark still. Twelve degrees below freezing.
Tremor along
the elegant, injured, right front

leg of the gelding on the cross-ties. Kneeling
girl.
The undersong of waters as she bathes

the leg in yet more cold. [tongue is broken]
[god to me]
Her hair the color of winter wheat.

Grammatical Mood

1.

There is, to her mind, only one.
        Or only
    one that's built to scale. Had they known

sooner. Had the only man to whom the CAT scan
        yielded
    so much detailed information not

been out of town that week. Had those few sticky
        platelets moved
    with just a shade more expedition through

the infant artery . . . The parallel life
        will not
    relent. But look, we may say to her, look

at them tied to their breathing machines, they do not
        cry
    (because of the tubes you'll say, you're right, to you

the silence is dreadful). To you the vicious
        calculus
    abides no counterargument: the oxygen

that supplements their unripe lungs destroys
        the retina,
           leaving the twice-struck child in darkness. What

must they think of us, bringing them into a world
        like this?

2.

        For want of an ion the synapse was lost.

For want of a synapse the circuit was lost.
        For want
           of a circuit, the kingdom, the child, the social

smile. And this is just one of the infinite means by which
        the world
           may turn aside. When my young daughter, whose

right hand and foot do not obey her, made us take
        off
           the training wheels, and rode and fell and pedaled

and fell through a week and a half of summer twilights
        and finally
           on her own traversed the block of breathing maples

and the shadowed street, I knew
        what it was like
           to fly. Sentiment softens the bone in its socket. Half

the gorgeous light show we attribute to the setting sun
        is atmospheric
           trash. Joy is something else again, ask Megan

on her two bright wheels.

      3.
             To live
        in the body (as if there were another

place). To graze among the azaleas (which are
          poison
        to humans, beloved by deer; not everything

the eye enjoys will sit benignly on the
          tongue). It must
        have been a head shot left her ear at that

frightening angle and the jaw all wrong,
          so swollen
        it's a wonder she can chew. Is that

where they aim, the good ones, when they're
          sober? At
        the head? At a doe? The DNR biologist is

saintly on the phone, though God knows he's not chiefly
          paid
        to salve the conscience (I have

bad dreams) of a gardening species stricken by
        its own
    encroachment. Fecundity starveth

the deer in the forest. It fouls the earth it
        feeds upon.
    Fecundity plants the suburban azalea, which

dies to keep the damaged deer in pain. I mean
        alive.

    4.

    For want of rain the corn was lost.

For want of a bank loan we plowed up the windbreak
        and burnt it
    (you must learn to think on a different scale, they told

us that). For want of a windbreak and rainfall
        and corn
    the topsoil rose on the wind and left. God's own

strict grammar (imperative mood). I meant
        to return
    to joy again. Just

give me a minute. Just look at the sky.

FROM *Magnetic North*

Sweet

Linda,
said my mother when the buildings fell,

before, you understand, we knew a thing
    about the reasons or the ways

    and means,
while we were still dumbfounded, still

bereft of likely narratives, *we cannot*
    continue to live in a world where we

    have so much
and other people have so little.

Sweet, he said.
    Your mother's wrong but sweet, the world

    has never self-corrected,
you Americans break my heart.

Our possum—she must be hungry or
    she wouldn't venture out in so

    much daylight—has found
a way to maneuver on top of the snow.

Thin crust. Sometimes her foot breaks through.
    The edge

    of the woods for safety or
for safety's hopeful look-alike. *Di-*

delphis, "double-wombed," which is
    to say, our one marsupial:

    the shelter then
the early birth, then shelter perforce again.

Virginiana for the place. The place
    for a queen

    supposed to have her maidenhead.
He was clever.

He had moved among the powerful.
    Our possum — possessed

    of thirteen teats, or so
my book informs me, quite a ready-made

republic — guides
    her blind and all-but-embryonic

    young to their pouch
by licking a path from the birth canal.

Resourceful, no? Requiring
    commendable limberness, as does

    the part I've seen, the part
where she ferries the juveniles on her back.

Another pair of eyes above
    her shoulder. Sweet. The place

    construed as yet-to-be-written-upon-
by-us.

And many lost. As when
    their numbers exceed the sources of milk

    or when the weaker ones fall
by the wayside. There are

principles at work, no doubt:
    beholding a world of harm, the mind

    will apprehend some bringer-of-harm,
some cause, or course,

that might have been otherwise, had we possessed
    the wit to see.

    Or ruthlessness. Or what? Or heart.
My mother's mistake, if that's

the best the world-as-we've-made-it
    can make of her, hasn't

    much altered with better advice. It's
wholly premise, rather like the crusted snow.

Bicameral

Choose any angle you like, she said,
the world is split in two. On one side, health

and dumb good luck (or money, which can pass
for both), and elsewhere . . . well,

they're eight days from the nearest town,
the parents are frightened, they think it's their fault,

the child isn't able to suck. A thing
so easily mended, provided

you have the means. I've always thought it was
odd, this part (my nursing school

embryology), this cleft in the world
that has to happen and has to heal. At first

the first division, then the flood of them, then
the migratory plates that make a palate when

they meet (and meeting, divide
the chambers, food

from air). The suture through which (the upper
lip) we face the world. It falls

a little short sometimes, as courage does.
Bolivia once, in May (I'd volunteer

on my vacations), and the boy was nine.
I know the world has harsher

things, there wasn't a war, there wasn't
malice, I know, but this one

broke me down. They brought him in
with a bag on his head. It was

burlap, I think, or sisal. Jute.
They hadn't so much as cut eyeholes.

2.

(Magdalena Abakanowicz)

Because the outer layer (mostly copper
with a bit of zinc) is good for speed

but does too little damage (what
is cleaner in the muzzle—you've begun

to understand—is also cleaner in
the flesh), the British at Dum Dum (Calcutta) devised

an "open nose," through which
the leaden core, on impact, greatly

expands (the lead being softer). Hence
the name. And common enough in Warsaw

decades later (it was 1943), despite
some efforts in The Hague. I don't

remember all of it, he wasn't even German,
but my mother's arm—

that capable arm—was severed at
the shoulder, made (a single

shot) a strange thing altogether.
Meat. I haven't been able since

to think the other way is normal, all
these arms and legs.

This living-in-the-body-but-not-of-it.

    3.

Sisal, lambswool, horsehair, hemp.
The weaver and her coat-of-many-

harrowings. If fiber found *in situ,* in
agave, say, the living cells that drink

and turn the sun to exoskeleton,
is taken from the body that

in part it constitutes (the
succulent or mammal and its ex-

quisite osmotics), is
then carded, cut, dissevered

in one fashion or another from
the family of origin, and

gathered on a loom,
the body it becomes will ever

bind it to the human and a trail
of woe. Or so

the garment argues. These
were hung as in an abattoir.

Immense (12 feet and more from upper
cables to the lowest hem). And vascular,

slit, with labial
protrusions, skeins of fabric like

intestines on the gallery floor.
And beautiful, you understand.

As though a tribe of intimates (the
coronary plexus, said the weaver) had

been summoned (even such
a thing the surgeon sometimes has

to stitch) to tell us, not unkindly, See,
the world you have to live in is

the world that you have made.

Make-Falcon

(Frederick II of Hohenstaufen, The Art of Falconry*)*

1.

Of the oil gland . . . Of the down . . .
            Of the numbers and arrangement
of feathers in the wing . . . I have seen
            on the plains of Apulia

how the birds in earliest spring were weak
            and scarcely able to fly.
Of the avian nostrils and mandibles . . . Of
            the regular sequence of molt . . .

Aristotle, apt to credit hearsay where
            experiment alone
can be relied upon, was wrong about
            the migrant column. Concerning

the methods of capture . . . the jesses . . .
            The swivel, the hood, the falcon's bell . . .

2.

The finest of them—here I mean
            for swiftness, strength,

audacity and stamina—are brooded
        on the Hyperborean cliffs (an island
chiefly made of ice). And I
        am told but have not ascertained

the farther from the sea they nest,
        the nobler will be the offspring.

    3.

Triangular needles are not to be used.
        The room

to be darkened, the bird
        held close in the hands of the assistant,
linen thread. By no means pierce
        the *membrana nictitans,* lying between

the eyeball and the outermost
        tissue, nor place the suture, lest it tear,
too near the edge. To seel,
        from *cilium,* lower lid,

which makes her more compliant to the falconer's
        will but also (I have
seen this in the lesser birds as well) more bold
        in flight. The senses

to be trained in isolation: taste,
              then touch, then hearing (so
the bars of a song she will evermore link to
                        food), and then the sight restored,

in order that the falcon may
              be partly weaned or disengaged from that
which comes by nature.
                    The falconer's purse or

carneria, owing
              to the meat it holds . . .
The carrier's arm . . . the gauntlet . . . the horse . . .
                    They greatly dislike the human face.

              4.

If you ask why the train is made of a hare,
              you must know no other flight
more resembles
              the flight at a crane than that

the falcon learns in pursuit of a hare
              nor is more beautiful.
Make-falcon: meaning
              the one who is willing

to fly in a cast with another less
              expert (the seasons
best suited . . . the weather . . . the hours . . .)
              and by example teach.

5.

The removal of dogs, which praise
          will better effect than will the harshest
threats, from the prey. Their reward.
          You must open

the breast and extract the organ that moves
          by itself, which is to say, the heart,
and let the falcon feed.
          The sultan

has sent me a fine machine combining
          the motions of sun and moon,
and Giacomo makes a poem of fourteen
          lines. The music is very good,

I think. (Of those who refuse to come to the lure ... Of
          shirkers ... Of bating ...)
But give me the falcon for art.

Bright Shadow

for Peter Davison

Wherever they come from whether the all-
　　　but-impenetrable bracken
　　　　　　on the nearer
　　　side of Maple Road (so closely does she bed

them down) or deeper in the wetland (each
　　　　　new season surrendering further to
　　　　　　the strangle
　　　of purple loosestrife) they

have made for weeks a daybed of
　　　　　the longer
　　　　　　　　grass beneath the net
　　　that sometimes of an evening marks

the compass of our shuttlecock
　　　　　so Steven
　　　　　　　　when at last he finds
　　　an afternoon for mowing must purposely

chase them into the woods where she
　　　　　so watchful
　　　　　　　　　in the normal course of foraging but
　　　lulled or made a stranger to her own

first-order instinct for dis-
                quietude (so firmly
                            have the scents and apparitions of
                this people-riddled bit of earth impressed

themselves upon the wax that stands for world-
                as-usual) (a scant
                            twelve months ago she was
                herself the sucking diligence that made

the mother stagger on the dew-drenched
                lawn) will find them near the salt lick and
                            as by a subtle field-of-
                force will reel them back to

stations-of-the-daily-path that portion out
                their wakefulness
                            (the ravaged
                rhododendrons bearing witness) forever en-

grafting the strictures of hunger (bright shoots)
                to the strictures (bright
                            shadow) of praise.

Father Mercy, Mother Tongue

If the English language was good enough for Jesus
            Christ, opined
     the governor of our then-most-populous

          state, *it is good enough for the schoolchildren*
                    of Texas.
     Which is why, said the man at the piano, I

will always love America: the pure
          products
     of the Reformation go a little crazy here.

                    Red bowl
                         of dust, correct us, we
               are here on sufferance every one.

     In 1935 the very earth rose up
                    against us, neither
          tub-soaked sheets nor purer thoughts could keep it

out. Doorsills, floorboards, nostrils,
                    tongue. The sugarbowl
          was red with it, the very words we spoke

were dirt.
There must have been something
to do, said my youngest one once (this
was worlds
away and after the fact).

We hoped for rain.

We harvested thistle to feed the cows.
We dug up soapweed. Then
we watched the cows and pigs and chickens die. *Red*
bowl
of words.

And found ourselves as nameless as
those poor souls up from Mexico

and just about as welcome as the dust.
Pity the traveler
camping by a drainage ditch in someone else's

beanfield, picking someone else's bean crop *who is here*
and gone.

And look

where all that parsing of the Latin led: plain Eunice
in her later years refused

to set foot in a purpose-
                              built church (a cross
              may be an idol so
                                                  a white-
              washed wall may be one too), preferring to trust

                        a makeshift circle of chairs in the parlor
                                                        (*harbor for*

              the heart in its simplicity),
                    her book.

                                                  This morning
              I watched a man in Nacogdoches calling
                              all of the people to quit

                                        their old lives, there were screens
                    within screens: the one

              above his pulpit (so huge
                              was the crowd), the one I worked
              with my remote. *Then turn* . . .

                        And something like the vastness of the parking lot
                              through which
              they must have come (so
                              huge) appeared
                                                  to be on offer, something

              shimmered like the tarmac on an August day.

Is this
the promised solvent? (Some were
weeping, they were black and white.)

A word

so broad and shallow (*Flee*), so rinsed
of all particulars (*Flee Babel,*

said the preacher) that translation's
moot. The tarmac
keeps the dust down, you must give it

that. The earth this time will have to scrape us off.

At the Window

Suppose, we said, that the tumult of the flesh
were to cease
and all that thoughts can conceive, of earth,
of water, and of
air, should no longer speak to us; suppose
that the heavens
and even our own souls were silent, no longer
thinking of themselves
but passing beyond; suppose that our dreams
and the visions
of our imagination spoke no more and that every
tongue and every sign
and all that is transient grew silent—for all
these things
have the same message to tell, if only we can
hear it, and
their message is this: We did not make ourselves,
but he
who abides forever made us. Suppose, we said,
that after giving
us this message and bidding us listen to him who
made them they
fell silent and he alone should speak to us,
not through them
but in his own voice, so that we should hear
him speaking,
not by any tongue of the flesh or by an angel's

voice, not in the
sound of thunder or in some veiled parable
but in his own voice,
the voice of the one for whose sake we love
what he has made;
suppose we heard him without these, as we two
strained to do . . .

And then my mother said, "I do not know why
I am here."
And my brother for her sake wished she might
die in her own
country and not abroad and she said, "See
how he speaks."
And so in the ninth day of her illness, in the
fifty-sixth year
of her life and the thirty-third of mine, at the
mouth of the Tiber

in Ostia . . .

The Turning

Just then, when already he's trying
      to leave, improbably

        young and fair-
complected, the absence of pigment a kind

of disease—he's come as a last
      concession and the church

      is cold, the other,
the pastor, so palpably wedded to grief he

looks with envy at the fair one, grief's
      addictive, it will hitch

      a ride on anything—
and that's when it happens, off-camera,

outside, some parting of the beaten
      sky as relayed

      by the gaffer, and
the window for a moment floods with not

that winter light from which the film, in English,
      takes its name but

winter scorched
by heaven's high contempt so that

the simplest among us may see and under-
stand: no help.

You dreary
Scandinavians, my husband says, your

serotonin uptake goes awry and you decide
it's metaphysical.

But isn't (I'll grant
the serotonin) isn't that just the point?

The cameraman makes his meticulous
case for the folds

of an eyelid, the decent
proportion of table and chair, the un-

remitting body of the world in all
its loveliness, and still

the one who suffers is
determined to be lost. He'd gladly

sell his unborn child for one decisive
scourging if

it meant
the one-who-scourges were for just

that instant forced to show his hand.
He's hopelessly

outmatched, of course,
the god of irony has such a long head start.

And therefore I think he stands for us,
the pallid one, though he

believes and we do not.
Though he has been punished once

for believing and once for despair, while we
confine our scruple to

the mise en scène.
He's all but gone. He will not live to see

another suppertime, the one
who was to be

his lifeline hasn't
any life to spare. And so he turns,

but barely, just the slightest
movement sideways

of his eyes, as though
to spare the one, the man

of God whose monstrous self-absorption is
        as lethal as a loaded

        gun, to spare him his own
iniquity. The turning

is a kind of tact, you see it still in
        country people,

        my uncle when
he visits always sits near the door so his boots

won't soil the kitchen. First
        the scorching then

        —the faithful
have a name for this—the ordinary cold.

My Father Comes Back from the Grave

for Karen

I think you must contrive to turn this stone
    on your spirit to lightness.

Ten years.
    And you, among all the things of the earth he took

to heart—they weren't so many after all—bent nearly
    to breaking with daily

        griefs. *The grass*
    beneath our feet. Poor blades. So

leaned on for their wavering homiletic (pressed for
    paltry, perpetual,

        raiment, return,
    the *look-for-me* every child appends to absence) it's

a wonder they keep their hold on green. *Come back*
    to me as grass beneath

        my feet. But he
    inclined to different metaphors.

                    *

        Your neighbor,

166

the young one, the one with two small boys, the one
who knew

what to do when the
gelding had foundered and everyone else was sick

with fear, can no longer manage the stairs on his own.
The wayward

cells (proliferant,
apt) have so enveloped the brain stem that

his legs forget their limberness. The one
intelligence

driving it all. The one
adaptable will-to-be-ever-unfolding that recklessly

weaned us from oblivion will
as recklessly have done

with us. *Shall the fireweed
lament the fire-eaten meadow?* Nothing

in nature (*whose roots make a nursery of ash*) (but
we . . .) so

parses its days in dread.

*

And in that other thing,   distinguishing

the species that augments itself with tools.
                    With

                    drill bits in
          the present case, with hammer, saw,

and pressure-treated two-by-eights: a ramp
                    for the chair

                    that wheels the one
          who cannot walk. He will not live to use

it much, a month perhaps, but that
                    part, o

                    my carpenter, you
          have never stooped to reckon. Now

the father, where does he come in? Whose
                    cigarette,

                    whose shot glass, whose
          broad counsel at the table saw ("I told

you not to do that") ever
                    freighted a daughter's learning.

Whose work
was the world of broken things and a principle

meant to be plain. The grass is mown? The people
in the house may hold

their heads up. Not?
A lengthening reproach. And thus

the shadow to your every move. The cough,
the catch, continuo: the engine

that breaches your scant four hours
of sleep. And what should you see (still

sleeping) as you look for the source of the sound?
Our father on the mower making

modest assault
on the ever-inadequate-hours-of-the-day, as

manifest in your neglected
lawn. Fed up, no doubt. Confirmed

in his private opinions. But
knightly in his fashion and—it's this

I want to make you see—
in heaven to be called upon.

Over Easy

Cloud cover like a lid on.
       Thwarted trees. And three more hours
of highway to be rid of. My darlings don't want
          a book on tape. They want

a little indie rock, they want to melt
       the tweeters, they want
mama in the trunk so they can have some un-
          remarked-on fun.

Fine. I've got my window, I can contemplate
       the flatness of Ohio. I can think
about the ghastly things we've leached into
          the topsoil, I can marvel that the

scabrous fields will still accept the plow. Except
       some liquid thing is happening just behind
the trees, some narrow sub-
          cutaneous infusion where

the darkening earth and darker strato-
       cumulus have not yet sealed
their hold. A pooling
          fed by needle drip: pellucid, orange,

a tincture I would almost call unnatural were
            it not so plainly nature-
born. Till what had been a stricken contiguity
            of winter-wasted

saplings starts to sharpen and distill, as though
            a lens had been adjusted or a mind
had cleared. *Our sorry dispersal,*
                  the Bishop of Hippo wrote

to his flock, *but the voice of a child*
            recalled me. When the girls were small
we took them to an island once, the sun
                  above the sea, and with

the other paying customers we'd watch it set.
            A yolk, I thought. The not-yet-
torn meniscus with its cunning corrective to
                  up and down. You've held

one in your palm no doubt: remember the weight?
            Remember the lemony slickness we so oddly
call "the white" and how it drains
                  between your fingers? *Not*

in chambering and wantonness the sun would swell
            nor strife and plumply flatten like
a yolk-in-hand. Would steep there in the salt-
                  besotted vapors till

we must have been watching an aftereffect,
        so quickly did it vanish. *Till*
the whole of expectation, wrote the bishop—this
            Ohio sky, the road, my noisy

darlings—*is exhausted and*—
        now mandarin, madder—*what was*
the future—cinnabar, saffron, marigold,
           quince—*becomes the past.*

Prodigal

Copper and ginger, the plentiful
    mass of it bound, half loosed, and
       bound again in lavish

    disregard as though such heaping up
were a thing indifferent, surfeit from
       the table of the gods, who do

       not give a thought to fairness, no,
    who throw their bounty in a single
lap. The chipped enamel—blue—on her nails.

The lashes sticky with sunlight. You would
    swear she hadn't a thought in her head
       except for her buttermilk waffle and

    its just proportion of jam. But while
she laughs and chews, half singing
       with the lyrics on the radio, half

       shrugging out of her bathrobe in the
    kitchen warmth, she doesn't quite
complete the last part, one of the

sleeves—as though, you'd swear, she
    couldn't be bothered—still covers
       her arm. Which means you do not

see the cuts. Girls of an age—
fifteen for example—still bearing
the traces of when-they-were-

new, of when-the-breasts-had-not-
been-thought-of, when-the-troublesome-
cleft-was-smooth, are anchored

on a faultline, it's a wonder they
survive at all. This ginger-haired
darling isn't one of my own, if

own is ever the way to put it, but
I've known her since her heart could still
be seen at work beneath

the fontanelles. Her skin
was almost otherworldly, touch
so silken it seemed another kind

of sight, a subtler
boundary than obtains for all
the rest of us, though ordinary

mortals bear some remnant too,
consider the loved one's fine-
grained inner arm. And so

it's there, from wrist to
elbow, that she cuts. She takes
her scissors to that perfect page, she's good,

she isn't stupid, she can see that we
who are children of plenty have no
excuse for suffering we

should be ashamed and so she is
and so she has produced this many-
layered hieroglyphic, channels

raw, half healed, reopened
before the healing gains momentum, she
has taken for her copy-text the very

cogs and wheels of time. *And as for
her other body,* says the plainsong
on the morning news, *the hole*

*in the ozone, the fish in the sea,
you were thinking what exactly? You
were thinking a comfortable*

breakfast would help? I think
I thought we'd deal with that tomorrow.
Then you'll have to think again.

Elegant

(C. elegans)

Dewpoint and a level field. Or slick
      of agar,

microscope,
          the embryonic roundworm and
an open mind. The world so rarely

          lets us in, let's
          praise

    the lucky vista when it does.
          We knew,
said my tutor, that death was a part of it, think

of the webbing that's eaten away in
          order
          that you may have fingers. We

          didn't know—how to put this?—before

we mapped our soil-borne roundworm, *C.*

      for *Caenor-* (filth) *hab-*
ditis (one who dwells there) with

its thousand and ninety invariant
                        cells of which
             131 and always
       the same

       and always in a particular sequence are programmed
for extinction,
                  we had no idea how close
              to the heart of it death
                            must be.
     At first
              a sort of cratered field, or
                         granulated—see it?—both

      the raised parts and con-
                  cavities, the sculpting
                           light,

and then a sort of swelling (it's a corpse now) then
            engulfment (that's
        the sister cell) and then

                        the disappearance (you'll
        remember how the lipids "lose their place").

   And on our chart an x where would

        be daughter cells, "a fate
        like any other." It's

a lie, of course, the light

    and shadow so disposed, a
                friendly
  lie, *as if* as in a play: of

          something less congenial to the seeing

      eye, the microscope
         makes shadow and
our question gains some traction and the world,

             though not
        just yet and not
           so seamlessly, makes sense.

Proprietary sequencing? Don't
    break my heart.

      We thought at first a camera
    would be just the thing, the thing itself in real
          time caught for anyone

  to stop
and start, but that

      was to ignore how much the camera
  misses, how what we call seeing

      in an ever-changing depth

of field while (twofold,
threefold, turning on its axis, still

unhatched) our worm

performs its complex cleavages and differentiations
is already
to have balanced on the scales

of thought. What
answered, what
the optics (see Nomarski) really
needed on the other end

was homely as the worm: a pencil,

paper, one man preternat-
urally good at this, and
thirteen hours,
a little more, from founder cell to hatching (let's say

coffee, lots). And found
he had transcribed there? Found

that death was not an afterthought. The genome
is a river too. And simpler, far

more elegant, to

keep the single system and discard the extra cells
                              it spawns. So *apo-*

(Gk., away from) *ptosis* (fall), as leaves

                        preserve the tree by learning
            to relinquish it. A river
                            of intelligence runs through us, could
        the part we do on purpose do

                    less harm. One version
of the lesson is its usefulness, the kindred
                    genes that help us break the circuit

        of malignancy, we name them for what happens when
                            they fail.
                        But use is not

        the whole of it. *He wants,* said my father (and this
                    of one he loved), *to live*

        forever, so I knew it was contemptible (had loved
    forever). Death
                        is not an afterthought nor

    (mother of beauty) will death
                        undone assist us, we
are made of it, are cognate (mother) to the worm, a worthy

                        daily labor and this thread
            of in-the-cells remembering make it so.

FROM *The Selvage*

The Selvage

1.

So door to door among the shotgun
shacks in Cullowhee and Waynesville in
our cleanest shirts and *ma'am*
and *excuse me* were all but second

nature now and this one woman comes
to the door she must have weighed
three hundred pounds Would you be
willing to tell us who you plan to vote

for we say and she turns around with
Everett who're we voting for? The
black guy says Everett. The black guy
she says except that wasn't the language

they used they used the word
we've all agreed to banish from even our
innermost thoughts, which is when
I knew he was going to win.

2.

At which point the speaker discovers,
as if the lesson were new,
she has told the story at her own expense.
Amazing, said my sister's chairman's

second wife, to think what you've
amounted to considering where you're from,
which she imagined was a compliment.
One country, friends. Where when

we have to go there, as, depend
upon it, fat or thin, regenerate
or blinkered-to-the-end, we shall,
they have to take us in. I saw

3.

a riverful of geese as I drove home across
our one-lane bridge. Four hundred of them
easily, close massed against the current and
the bitter wind (some settled on the ice) and just

the few at a time who'd loosen rank to
gather again downstream. As if
to paraphrase. The fabric
every minute bound

by just that pulling-out that holds
the raveling together. You were driving
all this time? said Steven. Counting
geese? (The snow falling into the river.)

No. (The river about
to give itself over to ice.) I'd stopped.
Their wingspans, had they not
been taking shelter here, as wide as we are tall.

Slight Tremor

The fine fourth finger
of his fine right hand,

just slightly, when
he's tracking our path

on his iPhone or
repairing the clasp

on my watch I
will not think about

the myelin sheath.
Slight tremor only,

transient, so
the flaw in the

pavement must
have been my

mother's back.

Constitutional

(O. G., 1872–1962)

It's a wonder they didn't all of them die of the
      sun those days. Remember
Ole's forehead and the backs of his hands?
The fair-haired sons of Norway in their bright
      Wisconsin fields, the map

of blessed second chances writ in tasseled
      corn. (The damage writ
in melanin.) I never could stand it, my father
would say, by which he meant the morning
      constitutional: the dose

of electric fencing Ole found was just the
      cure for frozen joints.
But joints be damned, the rest of it my father
loved, he'd cast about for a portion I
      could manage, maybe

Linda could fetch the cows. Poor man. He little
      thought how quickly
the race declines. *Ourselves and our posterity.*
It all alarmed me: dung slicks, culvert, swollen
      teats, the single narrow

wire above the barbed ones, commotion
       of flies on the rim
of the pail. We're better at living on paper,
some of us, better at blessings already
       secured. The fence?

It was for animals. And insulated, quaintly,
       with a species of porcelain
knob. That part, at least, I had the wit
to find benign, like the basket of straw-flecked
       eggs. A touch of homely

caution in the liable-to-turn-on-us world.
       Ordain and establish.
And breakable too. An old man at his battery-
charged devotions, double-fisted on
       the six-volt fence. *In order*

to form. A measure of guesswork, a measure
       of faithful retraining-from-
harm, let us honor the virtues of form.
And all the dead in company, if only
       not to shame them.

Lately, I've taken to

guessing a lot,
                chiefly in
the auditory realm, where I
am less and less

acute, which leads to masses
                of amusement
on the home front—Mom
                in orbit!—and what must

by now approximate
                a twenty-point
drop in the quotient we call
                IQ.

Endearing's not my
                strong suit
but I'll take what I can get.
                Forty percent

is what I thought I heard
                tonight but
surely that's not possible. All
                that ozone lost?

A single Arctic winter? I
        had thought
those were the healing months
      for snowpack, but it

seems the stratospheric ice
          does something
with the sunlight that's inim-
      ical. Unfriendly

in the long run to the cold.
        So cold
against itself. Which we
      have done. Which, if

I may compare great things to
        small, is what
my doctor thinks may be
      the trouble with my ear:

by-blow of the larger,
        chronic
proneness to construe what might
      have been benign

as something to be fought.
        So malleus,
stapes, hammer and tongs. I've
      seen the enemy and he . . .

etc. On an island in
        the Tyrifjord
in Norway several days ago,
     a man who said

he'd come for their protection
        and, what's
worse, who with a not-before-un-
     heard-of-in-the-history-

of-the-world excuse for
        logic really
thought that was the case,
     hunted down and shot

as many people as he could.
        Obsession
at the barricades, which when
     it goes wrong in the body

we label as autoimmune.
        The body ingenious.
Body so resilient he
     chose hollow-point bullets

to better his odds. At least,
        said the girl in the
newscast, he was one
     of us, and everyone knew

exactly what she meant.

Getting and Spending

(Isabella Whitney, "The maner of her Wyll")

I.

We're told it was mostly the soul
    at stake, its formal

        setting-forth, as over water,
where, against all odds,

the words-on-paper make
    a sort of currency, which heaven,

        against all odds, accepts.
So *Will*, which is to say, May what

I purpose, please, this once, and what
    will happen coincide.

        To which the worldly
dispositions were mere afterthought:

your mother's ring and so forth. What
    the law considered yours

        to give. Which in the case of
women was restricted—this was

long ago, and elsewhere—so
    that one confessedly "weak

of purse" might all the more
emphatically be thought of as having little

to say. Except about the soul. The late
disturbance in religion

having done that much, the each
for each responsible, even a servant,

even the poor. Wild, then—quite
beyond the pale—to hustle

the soul-part so hastily off
the page. And turn, our Isabella Whitney,

to the city and its faithlessness. Whose
smells and sounds—the hawker's cry,

the drainage ditch in Smithfield—all
the thick-laid, lovely, in-your-face-and-nostrils stuff

of getting-by no woman of even the slightest
affectation would profess to know,

much less to know so well.
As one would know the special places on

his body, were the passion merely personal.

2.

Wattle and brickwork. Marble and mud.
      The city's vast tautology. No city

      without people and no people but
will long for what the city says they lack:

high ceilings, gloves and laces, news,
      the hearth-lit circle of friendship, space

      for solitude, enough to eat.
And something like a foothold in the whole-of-it,

some without-which-not, some
      little but needful part in all the passing-

      from-hand-to-hand of it, so
every time the bondsman racks his debtor or

the shoemaker hammers a nail or one un-
      practiced girl imagines she

      has prompted a look of wistfulness,
a piece of it is yours because

your seeing it has made it that much slower
      to rejoin the blank

oblivion of never-having-
been. The year was fifteen hundred seventy-

three. The year of our Redeemer, as
they used to say. That other

circuit of always-in-your-
debt. From which she wrested, in her open

I-am-writing-not-for-fun-but-for-the-money
way of authorship, a world

not just of plenty but—and here's
the part that's legacy—of love.

Dido Refuses to Speak

I.

The forestays, the sternsheet,
                    the benches,
        the yard,

            the wooden pins to which
        the oars are
bound with strips of leather, he

        explained this, thole
and loom, I thought the words
                    were just as lovely as the

workings. And I thought
            I knew the principle:
        the moving forward facing where you've

            been, the muscled
        quarrel with the muscled sea, like
love, that sweet againstness. And

        the linen sail:
happy the weaver whose work might bedeck
                the chamber where we

lay us down. How strange
        it seems from just a little distance:
the living tree, the ax,

      the chisel, cattle
whom we kill and
skin, all so that they may live again on

water but including us.

2.

Because she'd never not
      been there, my Anna (I
can feel her now, the back

      of her hand as I hold it against
my eyelid, I have always loved
to touch with eyes), because

      her voice was all the traction I'd ever
required, because
      so long as earth contained

precisely
      that measure of temple to eyebrow,
eyebrow to lip, I knew

      I had a home, it was
my sister I made
to make the thing ready—the firewood in

its lofty escarpment, the torches,
the oil—and she, of course,
          when she asked what I meant to do,

to whom I lied. I meant
          my bitter heart to foul
          the wind that filled his sails. I did not ask

          what
          if the wind should change direction,
who would choke.

3.

As when in early summer in the fields
          of silver thyme, the bees
          are thick with happy industry . . .

          As when the workmen trust
          their overseer to be just . . .
As when the world was tuned to us and we

          the world, my city
on its quarried footing rose and rang with
          purpose and

the water loved its channels and the
          terraces their civic flight
          of stairs. Reluctant

evening, loath
to lose the sight of them, would finger
the vertical facings until they

blushed. I know
a better mind would not require
the elements

to be like us, we smear
our sorry longings on
the rocks and trees, but then

the very daylight
seemed to say we'd built to scale.

4.

Once in a narrow garden I
encountered a thing I'd known
before. A scent. I had

no words for it. Not citron,
though it bore that solvent
aptitude. Not anise, though it harbored

a touch of clay. A fragrance I
had known as in another life,
or this life, but before

the daily watering down. Which left me
half transported on an un-
distinguished plot of ground. So think

what it meant when he began to
speak. The story we'd stowed
as ballast on the fleeing ships, had painted

on our temple walls, the very lights
and darks we had depended on to make
the place less strange, and on

a stranger's lips. To whom
the story properly belonged. Or he
to it, is there a difference? And

poor Dido mere excursus for them both.

5.

If I burn the oars he won't be able to use them
to leave if I
lock up the winds in my cellar

if I shred the rigging or just
that pair of tendons at his inner
thigh not

so he suffers no but so he isn't able to
walk without help
                    and as for the eyes

he's already seen how I love him what need
                    for the eyes I was
          —wasn't I?—young when the

                    other one came to me dressed
          in his wounds which
wounds my brother gave him I

          have ever . . . in faithfulness since but
mistaken the . . . yes or lost
                    the thread and now

these swarming . . . whom I
                    welcomed as more of our own as
          on a carcass their indecent haste

                    their blackened . . . when I ought . . .
the tar-slicked hulls . . . And now
                    these trails of filthy mucus in the sand.

          6.

The child.
          I might
          except for the child have been

content.
But he in all his careless beauty—
cheekbone still untrammeled and the tidemark

of hair at his nape—he sat
beside me where we ate,
he laughed, his every un-

selfconscious bit of lassitude or
fervor was
a manifest that pled the father's case.

There is no
outside to such arguments.
And surely I took precautions? What

was true for me ought doubly to
have been the case for one whose
future he

secured. So hostage both.
All three. And now
I'm told he wasn't a

child at all but a
god in the shape of a child.
Redundant.

7.

Wasn't it nearly too sweet to be borne,
              that motherwit
       bought me a kingdom. *Every inch*

              that will fit in the oxhide.
       Which I shaved so fine,
in strips of such exquisite near-

transparency, we thought the whole
of Africa might fall within our
              grasp. So dredged

the ports and felled the woodlands in the
              heady tide
       of heaven's bright approval . . .

       I am glad to find
       they haven't cut the woodland here.
Give me a margin of shadow, I'll tell you

       no lies. The myrtle
suits me, understory to
              the last, and mutes those sounds of

sorrow from the river. Not a single
              pine, no
       striving toward the masthead or the

roofbeam, just
these little purple blossoms, which
I do not take ironically.

And best: the plates of silver
bark, which must be
what happens to words.

From the Life of Saint Peter

(Brancacci Chapel, Florence)

I. HIS SHADOW

They brought us out on the pavement then,
our pallets
and cots, the
poorest barely decent in their bedclothes.
And facing

as best we could the sun,
so whether
he would or no his passing shadow might
pass over us and we
be healed. As if

some ghastly catalogue of everything you
fear the flesh
might one day have in store for you should
suddenly block
your way back home.

But look
how the painter has lovingly rendered the clubs
of my knees. Gall-
knots, hooves
of callus you would surely look away from in the

ordinary
course of things, calves
like an afterthought trailing behind. I wonder
will I get to keep some sign of this when I'm made
whole.

I've come to think
the body scorns hypothesis, hasn't it
paid for its losses
in kind? While we are writ in water. My
advantage here

was learning so early how little the world will
spare us. Now
this rumored cure:
You see
the peeling fresco? It was once as chaste as you.

2. THE DEATH OF ANANIAS

There must have been something with-
                          held as if
you know the story you'll
              know has been said about me.

I saw what we all saw: goats and cattle,
                          grain,
an ancient and three newer family
              houses and finally

the second-best vineyard for miles around
                         converted
into silver and simply
              laid on the ground at their feet.

And namely the one called Peter: how
                         is it
that one among equals will seem
              to have harnessed the moon

and stars. I understood the next
                         part, how the
logic went: we hadn't been
              savages all our lives, we'd helped

the poor before. But this was something
                         else, was like
the dizzying vista above the gorge:
              you think you've been quite

happy, your loved ones are waiting to
                         welcome you
home and you can taste the broken rocks
              below through all your broken

teeth, you know the terror won't be
                         over until
you've thrown your one allotted life
              away. And so

I stepped back, just a little, from the
                    edge.
What kind of reckoning after all requires
        this all-or-nothing? Hadn't I

torn the lovely acres from my heart?
                    Which he
esteemed as so much filth. The least
        that would keep the cold off, that's

all I'd intended to put aside. You
                    see?
And cold came up to seize me.

3. THE TRIBUTE MONEY

Then, said my Master, *are the children
        free.* Which you might think
                would tell us what to do

        but we had caught the scent
of parable. So hook, so fish, the
                money in its mouth,

            the mucus and blood
        on the money. I paid the collector
as I'd been told and part

was the lesson and part was speaking
        truth to power and still
                there's part left over.

From whom, he said, do the kings
of the earth extract their tribute?
                Shining in its mouth as

                shines the golden hair
        you see to my left in the picture. From
the stranger, we said. But he

my Master loved said nothing, nothing
        but beauty was ever required
                of him. *Then are*

        the children free. Now look,
I'm not immune to this, I like
                to work the likeness out:

                for *pieces of money* read
        gifts of the earth, for *hook*
read *yours for the asking.* But as to

the one with golden hair, read what?
        That some shall leap while others
                crawl? That even

the best of love is partial?
The fish that flashed a thousand
            colors, though you throw

            him back, will drown.
Which makes me think
the gills in their air-scorched frenzy must

extract some tribute too.

4. THE EXPULSION

(with: *The Earthly Paradise,
Saint Peter in Prison, Saint Peter Released*)

So whether you read from left
            to right (sent howling

            from the garden where
the stories all begin) or simply

wander as gaps in the crowd
            permit, the pillars of the

            chapel will have told you
how to navigate. On one side

the pair of them driven like
            cattle, her face with its

sockets of grief. And on
the other side the premise still

unspoilt. Or is it promise? Where
the sword and angel

haven't yet obscured
the sky. You're thinking it's all

been lost on me, you've smiled
to find me sleeping while

the prisoner goes free.
But some must rest while others

watch, I've sorted the whole thing
out. Four panels, yes?

A child could do the
algebra: made free, in chains, in

chains, made free. Remorse, which
you call history, set

in motion by the paradox.
How many people contribute as

much? My sword, unlike the angel's,
sheathed, my charge an open

door. The saint required to
suffer where you see him, extramurally.

5 · THE BAPTISM OF THE
NEOPHYTES

He knelt because the others knelt. And
        nothing was odd about that except,
unlike the others, he seemed to know

nothing of shame. Which quite astonished
        me. Not brazened-it-out, or
wrapped-himself-in-pridefulness (the surest

sign of struggle), simply free, by what
        conjunction of insight or
ignorance I am still at a loss to imagine,

from the universal misery of fitting-in-
        the body. We were many
on the hillside, the waters ran shallow

for him as for everyone else, we thought
        this meant nothing to hide.
And it was then I knew the messenger.

For some of us, the treachery's half the
        getting there, we have to be
flayed by our own bad faith. And hence

the scene of washing. You'll remember
     we still thought it had no
limit, that the water and the air it came

from came unendingly, and clean.
     We thought we had fouled
ourselves alone. And then the young one

came and knelt and I could see
     the whole equation, what
we'd gained by it and what we had agreed

to lose. We'd meant to do better by
     those who came after,
that was both the pity and the point.

Her Argument for the Existence of God

This one then: the
doctor, who of course possesses a foreign name, thus
                            gathering all our what
shall we call them our powers of foreboding in a single

sordid corner of
the morning news, contrived to miss the following:
                            eight fractured ribs,
three missing fingertips, infected tissue, torn and partly

healed again,
between the upper lip and gum and, this you have to use
                            your Sunday
finest to imagine, a broken back, third lumbar, which

had all
but severed the spinal cord leaving him "floppy," or so
                            the coroner later
determined, below the waist. Now granted, she might not have

thought to expect
a wailing one-and-a-half-year-old to toddle obligingly
                            over the tiles nor
felt she had the leisure to apply her little mallet just below the

knee, we see that, but
we are not talking nuance here. The tooth he had swallowed, so
                            hard had been

the blow to his face—of course one had no inkling, that would

take some sort of
psychic or an MRI. But ulcerated lesions on the scalp and
                                        ears? I tell you if
I hear once more how the underage mother's underage boyfriend

suffered a difficult
childhood himself I'll start to wreck the furniture. When I'm
                                allowed to run the world you'll
have to get a license just to take the course on parenting and

everyone
will fail it and good riddance we'll die out. But in the
                                meantime which
is where we're always stranded and ignoring consolation

which is laughable what's
to be made of the sheer bad fit? The reigning brilliance
                                of the genome and
the risen moon. The cell wall whose electric charge forms now

a channel now
a subtle barrier no modulating thought has thought
                                to equal. The
arachnid's exoskeleton. The kestrel's eye. And we who might

have been worthy but
for reasons forever withheld from us aren't. Wouldn't you
                                rather be damned
for cause?

Still Life

1.

His ears his mouth his
    nostrils having filled

    with ash, his cheekbones
chin (all ash) and on the ash a tide

of seawrack that cannot
    be right a trail of scum or

    vomit then and either
his shoulder's been crushed by the

blast or angled on the stretcher so
    oddly that raising

    his arm to ward us off
he seems to be more damaged than he

is, and eyes
    that should have cracked the

    camera. This was not
the current nightmare this was two

or three nightmares ago, the men
    were loading plums and

peaches onto trucks at
Qaa. And though in my lucky and

ignorant life I have never so much as
 encountered the scent

 of explosives (I
had taken a different bus that day,

the city I live in is thicker with
 doctors than all of Beka'a

 is thick with bombs), I've
seen those eyes before exactly.

Failures of decency closer to home.

 2.

(The clearing of the ghetto)

Red wool, and falsely brightened, since
 we need the help.

 A child because
the chambers of the heart will hold so

little. If the filmmaker, having
 apprenticed in fables,

proposes a scale for which,
he hopes, we're apt and if

this bigger-than-a-breadbox slightly-
        smaller-than-the-microwave is

        just about the vista we can
manage, let's agree to call it history, let's

imagine we had somehow seen its face
        in time. But where

        in all of Kraków is
the mother who buttoned her coat?

A city steeped in harm-to-come,
        the film stock drained

        to gray. The sturdy
threading-forward of a child who

might be panicked by the crowd but
        has her mind now on

        a hiding place. Our
childlike conviction that she shall be

spared. Mistake that brings
        the lesson home: we lack

retention.
Chalk mark on a clouded screen.

3.

But what was it like, his dying?
It was like

     a distillation.
You had morphine? We had

morphine, but he couldn't use
     the bed. *The bed?*

     His lungs were so
thickened with tumors and phlegm

he had no way of breathing there.
     You'd rented the bed?

     He climbed down beside it
and asked for his tools. When something

was broken he fixed it, that had
     always been the way with him.

     So then . . . We left him in his
chair. But as the day went on we thought

he needed bedding so we tried to
     lift him. That's the once

he blamed us. *That's
the look you meant*. The why-

can't-you-people-just-leave-me-alone,
the where-is-your-sense-

of-shame. I will
remember it until I die myself.

You meant well. Meaning well
was not enough.

We meant that he
should know this wasn't lost on us.

The urn that holds his ashes does
a better job.

4.

Sister partridge, brother hare.
The linen on the table

with its hemstitch. I
have read the books on pridefulness:

the bounty of game park and sideboard
and loom, the ships

that brought the lemon trees,
the leisure that masters the view. But

I have come to think
        the argument-by-likeness makes

        a simpler point. The lemon,
for example, where the knife has been:

the pores, the pith, the luminescent
        heart of it, each differential

        boundary bound to open.
Meaning death, of course, the un-

protected flesh about to turn, but just
        before the turn, while looking

        can still be an act of praise.
I see you in the mirror every morning

where you wait for me. The linen,
        Father, lemon, knife,

        the pewter with its lovely
reluctance to shine. As though

the given world had given us
        a second chance.

NOTES

New Poems

"The Wrath of Juno (A wandering husband)"
Metamorphoses III: 359–401.

"The Weavers"
Metamorphoses VI: 26–145.

"The Dolphins"
Metamorphoses III: 582–691.

"The Wrath of Juno (It's the children)"
Metamorphoses IX: 280–315; III: 259–315; IV: 416–530.

"Pythagorean"
"It came to me . . .": Metempsychosis, or the transmigration of souls. See Leopold Bloom to Molly. Xenophanes tells the story of Pythagoras intervening on behalf of a dog being beaten in the street, claiming to recognize in its cries the voice of a departed friend.

"Ceres Lamenting"
Section 3: *Nirbhaya,* developed by actors in Mumbai under the direction of Yael Farber, responds to the gang rape and murder of Jyoti Singh Pandey in Delhi, December 2012.

FROM *Fire in the Conservatory*

"*De Arte Honeste Amandi*"
Andreas Capallanus, *The Art of Courtly Love*

"Maudlin; or, The Magdalen's Tears"
Georges de La Tour (1593–1642) painted the penitent Magdalen at least four times. But the speaker misremembers: the bare shoulder and the mirror appear in separate canvases.

"Eyes Like Leeks"

This poem is for Daniel Evans, who played Francis Flute who played Thisby in *A Midsummer Night's Dream,* Stratford-upon-Avon, 1994. And also for Archie Brechin.

"Maculate"

Most of the italicized passages in this poem are adapted from Luke 12.

"The Horses Run Back to Their Stalls"

This poem is dedicated to Jens Jensen, and to John D. Hertz, who gave him another job.

The nursery rhyme the speaker has in mind begins, "Ding dong bell / Pussy's in the well. . . ."

"Waterborne"

DNR: Department of Natural Resources.

"Pass Over"

The film referred to in section 2 is P. T. Anderson's *Magnolia.*

"Narrow Flame"

The title and bracketed phrases are from Sappho, fragment 31.

FROM *Magnetic North*

"Bicameral"

Sections 2 and 3 are based upon the work of the Polish artist Magdalena Abakanowicz (b. 1930) and on interviews published in Barbara Rose, *Magdalena Abakanowicz.* New York: Harry Abrams, 1994. The exhibit described in section 3, "Atelier 72," was mounted at the Richard Demarco Gallery in Edinburgh, August 1972.

"Make-Falcon"

Frederick II of Hohenstaufen (1194–1250), Holy Roman Emperor, King of Sicily and Jerusalem. Student of mathematics, natural history, architecture, and philosophy. Crusader, falconer, poet. Founder of the University of Naples. Patron to Giacomo (also called Jacopo) da Lentino (fl. 1215–33), generally credited with the invention of the sonnet.

"Father Mercy, Mother Tongue"

"If the English language . . .": Miriam "Ma" Ferguson, governor of Texas, 1924–26.

"At the Window"

The *Confessions* of St. Augustine, Book IX, trans. R. S. Pine-Coffin.

"The Turning"

Ingmar Bergman, *Winter Light* (*Nattvardsgästerna*), 1962. Cinematographer, Sven Nyqvist.

"Elegant"

In 2002 the Nobel Prize in physiology was awarded to Sydney Brenner, Robert Horvitz, and John Sulston for discoveries concerning "genetic regulation of organ development and programmed cell death." *C. elegans* was the model organism used in their research. My thanks to Nelson Horseman for calling my attention to this beautiful work, to John Sulston for sharing with me the text of his Nobel lecture, and, above all, to Ron Ellis for his patient and generous tutelage.

FROM *The Selvage*

"Lately, I've taken to"

Forty percent: Unfortunately, what the speaker heard was correct. NASA studies confirm an unprecedented forty percent loss in the ozone layer above the northern Arctic in the winter of 2010–11.

An island in the Tyrifjord: In order to "save Norway and Western Europe from a Muslim takeover," Anders Behring Breivik in July of 2011 killed sixty-nine members of the Norwegian Workers' Youth League, who were attending a retreat on Utøya Island. The Youth League is, in Breivik's view, too friendly to immigrants.

"Dido Refuses to Speak"

The child: In Marlowe's version of the story, Cupid assumes the guise of Ascanius, son of Aeneas, and touches Dido's breast with his golden arrow. The oxhide: For this account, see Marcus Junianus Justinus, *Epitome of the Philippic History of Pompeius Trogus*, Book XVIII. "Dido Refuses to Speak" was originally written as part of a commission for composer Susan Botti and the Blakemore Trio and premiered, as section 3 of *The Gates of Silence*, in Nashville and New York, February/March 2010.

"From the Life of Saint Peter"

His Shadow: Acts 5:15. The Death of Ananias: Acts 5:1–10. The Tribute Money: Matthew 17:24–27. The Expulsion / Saint Peter Released from Prison: Genesis 3:22–24 / Acts 12:6–10. The Baptism of the Neophytes: Acts 2:37–41.

"Still Life"

Section 2: *Schindler's List*, directed by Steven Spielberg, 1993.

INDEX OF TITLES AND FIRST LINES